businessbuddies

successful
finance for managers

For further success in all aspects of
business, be sure to read these other
businessbuddies books:

businessbuddies

successful
finance for
managers

Ken Lawson, M.A., Ed.M.

BARRON'S

First edition for the United States, its territories and dependencies, and Canada
published 2007 by Barron's Educational Series, Inc.

Conceived and created by
Axis Publishing Limited
8c Accommodation Road
London NW11 8ED
www.axispublishing.co.uk

Creative Director: Siân Keogh
Editorial Director: Anne Yelland
Design: Sean Keogh, Simon de Lotz
Consulting Editor: Ken Lawson
Production: Jo Ryan

NOTE: The opinions and advice expressed in this book are intended as a guide only. The publisher
and author accept no responsibility for any loss sustained as a result of using this book.

All inquiries should be addressed to:
Barron's Educational Series, Inc.
250 Wireless Boulevard
Hauppauge, New York 11788
www.barronseduc.com

Library of Congress Control No: 2006932160

ISBN-13: 978-0-7641-3702-0
ISBN-10: 0-7641-3702-6

Printed and bound in China
9 8 7 6 5 4 3 2 1

contents

Introduction

If you've ever wondered just how business moves forward—or if you'd like to be one of the strategy wizards that moves business forward—you'll need to form a lasting, loving relationship with The Numbers. No matter how hot or innovative your company's product may be, no matter how ripe the market is for the new service your organization is offering, it's The Numbers that will ultimately spell success or disaster.

Successful Finance for Managers is your Book of Numbers. It outlines and explains the essential concepts, principles, strategies, and scenarios for lasting business success. If you've never studied what pushes a business through the four stages of a business cycle, this is the place to begin. If you need to bone up on the essentials of accounting, financing, and taxation, this is your single-stop resource. When you need to tour the terrain of business finance to explore its myriad ins and outs, this is your guidebook.

With writing that's clear, concise, and credible, *Successful Finance for Managers* provides you with a practical grounding in the art and science of business finance. Chapter 1 explains the fundamental principles of accounting. You'll read about its many benefits, and about the criteria for an effective accounting system. Then, you'll learn about the various types of business assets and the different kinds of depreciation that apply to all businesses, whatever their core activity or client base. Also explained are cash-basis accounting, goodwill, cost accounting, and accounting for leases.

In Chapter 2 you'll review basic concepts and terminology and learn how they're applied in typical business settings. You'll read a case study that analyzes the income statement of a company. Then, as you get rolling, you'll develop an understanding of liquidity, profitability, and solvency ratios.

Introduction continued

In Chapter 3 you'll find the how's and why's of financing daily business operations. Read how to create and stick to a budget, and why it's essential to business vitality. Learn how to understand your company, define objectives, and set financial targets. Gain an understanding of how to formulate and reach key objectives for a start-up business. Chapter 4 explains financing growth through the four stages of a business life cycle and recounts the success story of Amazon.com to illustrate how the right financing can make a business sing in a relatively short time.

Chapter 5 shows managers how to interpret financial data. It explains how to evaluate business performance, mark return on investment, and perform a breakeven analysis. You'll also learn about valuing the company in terms of "hard" and "soft" numbers, intangible assets, and market competition. Finally, in Chapter 6, you'll find a primer on taxes and taxation, including explanations of the various types of business structure, key business tax issues, as well as credits and deductions.

Successful Finance for Managers is a valuable resource for the key players in business. With the principles, concepts, and strategies explained in these pages, you'll gain an understanding of finance that will expand your knowledge and enhance your managerial capability. You'll see once and for all what makes business tick, how ultimate success is measured, and how you might help your company reach it faster. It's a Book of Numbers for you to live by.

Ken Lawson, M.A., Ed.M.
Career Management Consultant
New York

principles of accounting

An overview of accounting

WHAT IS IT?

Accounting describes a company's bookkeeping system: a record of money coming in and out of the business. The heart of modern financial accounting, which dates back to medieval Europe (some say even Ancient Greece), is that at least two entries have to be made for every transaction: a debit in one account and a corresponding credit in another account. This makes it easy to check for errors.

BENEFITS OF ACCOUNTING

1

Bookkeeping enables decision makers to use financial information to make proactive rather than reactive decisions.

2

Tracking financial information provides transparency for managers, investors, and creditors. In the United States, poor accounting also played an important role in the Enron and Worldcom scandals.

3

It keeps businesses out of jail. Bookkeeping is legally required in the United States particularly for tax-reporting purposes (see pp. 204–213).

CRITERIA FOR AN EFFECTIVE ACCOUNTING SYSTEM

1 It has to be accurate. A test of reliability is that independent auditors reach similar results.

2 It has to be relevant, providing managers, investors, and creditors alike with necessary information.

3 It has to be comparable so that users can easily compare the financial statements with those of other companies.

4 It has to be consistent. The same methods should have been applied across different periods and any change in methods fully explained.

5 It has to be user friendly: use an easy to use and read software package.

6 It has to be up to date and available so decisions can be made on time.

principles of accounting

GAAP

WHAT ARE THEY?
GAAP stands for "generally accepted accounting principles" that companies should conform to when tracking transactions and preparing financial statements.

ARE THEY ENFORCED?
The U.S. government does not enforce accounting principles, leaving rules and procedures to the self-regulating Financial Accounting Standards Board (FASB). The U.S. Securities and Exchange Commission (SEC) expects all publicly traded companies to follow GAAP. Publicly traded companies must be audited by a certified public accountant. The four biggest auditors are the multinationals Deloitte Touche Tohmatsu, Ernst & Young, KPMG, and PricewaterhouseCoopers.

FEATURES OF GAAP
GAAP's list of basic assumptions and principles include the following:

1 The company will be in operation for a long time to make future predictions possible and accurate.

2 The company will record its operations across different periods such as months, quarters, and years.

3 The company will record figures in a stable currency, namely the U.S. dollar.

4 Records of assets and liabilities will be based on historic, acquisition costs rather than fair market value, to ensure objectivity.

5 Companies should record revenue when agreements and invoices are signed, not when the cash is actually received (see pp. 56–61).

6 The company's revenues and expenses should be kept separate from the owners' personal expenses.

7 Expenses should match revenues when possible to demonstrate that the expense is making its contribution to revenue. Common exceptions to this rule are ongoing costs such as salaries and administration since it is more difficult to quantify their direct contribution to revenue.

Accrual-basis accounting

There are two basic accounting methods: accrual-basis accounting and cash-basis accounting.

ACCRUAL ACCOUNTING

WHAT IS IT?

Accrual-basis accounting records revenues and expenses when they are incurred, regardless of the actual period when cash is exchanged (which may be long delayed). A typical example is a sale on credit. The sale is registered when the invoice is generated rather than when the cash is collected. In the same way, an expense is recorded when materials are ordered rather than when they are actually paid for.

WHEN DO YOU USE THE ACCRUAL METHOD?

1 The accrual method is compulsory if the company sales are over $10 million (until recently $5 million), which covers most companies of any size.

2 Accrual is also used if the company is structured as a corporation (see pp. 194–198).

3 Businesses that have an inventory (see pp. 24–27) must use the accrual method. This will automatically apply to manufacturers, wholesalers, retailers, and certain publishers.

4 When a company sells on credit, using the accrual method matches income and expenses more accurately in any given time period.

Accrual-basis accounting continued

PROS

1 Accrual-basis accounting complies with GAAP, whereas cash-basis accounting does not.

2 Accrual-basis accounting provides a more complete picture of business performance because more transactions have to be recorded. A manager can instantly see what is going out and coming in to the business.

CONS

1 Standard accrual-basis financial statements (profit statements and balance sheets) do not indicate the cash inflows and outflows of a company.

2 Accrual-basis accounting is generally considered more expensive because it requires the bookkeeper to record a lot more transactions. However, in recent years, the development of accounting software has made the difference between the reporting methods less significant.

Cash-basis accounting

WHAT IS IT?

Cash-basis accounting registers financial events based on cash flows and cash position. Revenue is recognized only when cash is received, rather than when a client or supplier promises to make a payment. Similarly, expense is recognized when cash exchanges hands.

As a result, revenues and expenses are also called cash receipts and cash payments.

WHEN DO YOU USE CASH-BASIS ACCOUNTING?

1 When you are operating a small, cash-based business or a small service company.

2 If you are operating as a sole proprietor or sole trader (see pp. 190–191).

3 If you have a business with no inventory (most typically a service company).

PROS

1 The cash method is the most simple in that the books are kept based on the actual flow of cash in and out of the business. This is logged on a daily basis.

2 From a tax standpoint, a new company benefits from the cash method of accounting because recording income can be put off until the next tax year, but expenses are counted right away.

CONS

1 If you are a start-up company that is keen to record growing revenue, you are limited by the fact that you can only record actual, not projected, income.

2 For the creditors and stockholders of large enterprises, cash-basis accounting is financially inadequate because it fails to meet two of GAAP's basic principles: namely, that revenue should be recognized when it is realized and that revenue should be matched to expenses when possible.

Business assets

WHAT ARE THEY?

Business assets, according to the definition by the International Accounting Standards Board (IASB), are a "resource controlled by the enterprise as a result of past events and from which future economic benefits are expected to flow to the enterprise."

HOW DO YOU CLASSIFY THEM?

GAAP requires assets to be classified into certain divisions:

1 CURRENT ASSETS

Current assets include cash as well as other assets that the company expects to convert to cash or trade in any manner in the next operating cycle. They include:

- currency, deposits account, money orders, checks, bank drafts
- inventory (raw materials, components used in the normal business of the company)
- short-term investments such as securities
- receivables—these are usually reported as net of allowance for uncollectible accounts
- prepaid expenses

2 LONG-TERM INVESTMENTS
These include:

- investments in securities like long-term notes, bonds, common stock
- investments in fixed assets not used in day-to-day operations (like land)
- investments in funds such as pension or sinking funds
- investments in subsidiary or affiliated companies

3 FIXED ASSETS
These assets cover machinery, furniture, tools, land, and buildings. Except for land, which usually appreciates in value, these assets can be written off against profits by charging depreciation.

4 INTANGIBLE ASSETS
These include franchises, copyrights, patents, trademarks, and goodwill.

5 OTHER ASSETS
These include property held for sale, long-term prepaid expenses, and long-term receivables.

principles of accounting

Accounting inventory

This section covers the way some of your business assets are accounted for. Key areas include inventory, depreciation of fixed assets, and goodwill.

ACCOUNTING INVENTORY

WHAT IS IT?

Accounting inventory is the process of tracking down all the elements that make up the typical production process of most companies that sell products, whether they are manufacturers, wholesalers, or retailers. Such inputs include such items as raw materials, supplies, goods in various stages of production (work in process), and finished products.

WHY IS IT NECESSARY?

1

All companies that stock inventory are legally required to use the accrual method of accounting. Inventory appears as a current asset on an organization's balance sheet because the business can turn it into cash by selling it. Inventory is reported at the amount paid to obtain the merchandise, not at its selling price.

2

Companies that sell products need an effective system to record each inventory item to ensure there are sufficient supplies in stock to keep up with customer demand; to find out which items sell well or badly; and how long each item takes to produce.

3

Inventory records allow companies to track down the material cost associated with each item sold. Aside from the cost of acquisition, inventory brings associated costs for space, for utilities, and for insurance to cover staff, fire, and theft.

principles of accounting

Accounting inventory continued

COST FLOW ASSUMPTIONS

These are the three common assumptions that companies can choose to use consistently to classify inventory. Note that the costs can flow out of inventory in a different order from which the goods are physically removed from inventory.

1

AVERAGE COST
You calculate the cost of the item in the beginning inventory to which you add the cost of freight and taxes. You calculate the average by adding the beginning cost inventory for each month plus the ending cost inventory for the last month in the period. You divide by the number of months in the period for an average cost.

2 FIFO
FIFO (first-in, first-out) involves taking the first unit that arrived in inventory and transferring it to the cost of the first item sold.

3 LIFO
LIFO (last-in, first-out) considers the last unit arriving in inventory and the first one sold. Using LIFO, a company generally reports lower net income and lower book value. As this skews the value of inventory, resulting in lower taxation, GAAP has effectively banned LIFO.

principles of accounting

Depreciation

WHAT IS IT?

Most of a company's fixed assets like machinery, equipment, and vehicles (but not land) tend to decline in value over their lifetime use, generally five years or more. Depreciation is an average or expected view of this decline in value of an asset. For instance, if your company buys new office equipment, including computers, for a renovation, it cannot deduct the cost of these assets in its bookkeeping to enjoy an immediate tax benefit.

The company must instead depreciate the cost over the useful life of the asset.

In the case of a computer, the company can make calculations over five years, taking a tax deduction for a part of the cost each year. The company will use a far longer time span—say, 30 years—for an office or manufacturing facility than for a computer.

Under U.S. income tax regulations, the maximum allowable useful life is 40 years.

WHY IS IT NECESSARY?

1

Accounting standards bodies have detailed rules on which methods of depreciation are acceptable, and auditors will check that a company's assumptions underlying the estimates are fair. For instance, some pieces of equipment may depreciate by 10 percent a year; others, particularly in a rapidly developing technological sector, at a higher rate.

2

Depreciation is an example of applying the matching principle required under GAAP whereby a company matches its expenses with the income generated through the expenses, as laid down in generally accepted accounting principles.

3

A fair calculation of depreciation will ensure that the asset values in the balance sheet are not overstated. The value of an asset when it is bought will vary significantly after five years.

principles of accounting

Depreciation continued

HOW TO CALCULATE DEPRECIATION

There are several methods for calculating depreciation, generally based on either the passage of time or the level of activity (or use) of the asset. The three main ones are:

1

STRAIGHT-LINE DEPRECIATION

This is the simplest and most commonly used technique by companies. It works by taking first the purchase cost of the asset, for instance a computer—$1500—and estimating the cost of the computer in five years time when you have to dispose of it because it has become virtually obsolete. Known as the "salvage value," this cost is estimated at $150, which means the computer has depreciated by $1350. Divided by five years (the useful life of the computer), this means the computer depreciates by $270 a year.

If eventually the computer is sold for more than the salvage value, then the company has to declare capital gains to the tax office. However if the sales price is less than the salvage value, the capital loss becomes tax deductible.

2

DECLINING-BALANCE DEPRECIATION

This is a slightly more complicated method of fixed-asset depreciation as you don't just work an average depreciation value over the five years as in straight-line depreciation. Instead, you also factor in your estimates that the rate at which the computer loses its value is far higher in the first couple of years than toward the end. This means that the company accountant has to make depreciation calculations for each year by basing each year's depreciation on the previous year's net book value and its estimated useful life.

The tax benefits of declining-balance depreciation are greater because the depreciation expenses are higher in the early years of the asset's life.

3

ACTIVITY DEPRECIATION

This method differs from the two other methods because it doesn't take the lifetime of the asset into account but focuses on the asset's level of activity. A car is a good example because its lifetime will depend on its level of activity. For instance, if the car can run a maximum of 40,000 miles, it may use this up in two years or six years, depending on its activity level.

principles of accounting

Accounting for leases

WHAT IS IT?

When you lease equipment, office space, or a car, you are effectively renting an asset for a specified period of time in return for a stipulated, and generally periodic, cash payment.

TWO TYPES OF LEASES

1 OPERATING LEASE

With this type of lease, a company doesn't have to record the leased product or premise as an asset or liability on the income statement. You simply record the monthly check paid to the leasing company as a rent expense.

2 CAPITAL LEASE

This type of lease is recorded as both an asset and a liability on the financial statements, generally at the present value of the rental payments.

WHICH TYPE OF LEASE?

The Financial Accounting Standards Board (FASB) provides criteria for when a lease should be capitalized:

1 When the lessor transfers ownership of the asset to the lessee.

2 When the lessee signs a "bargain purchase option" that allows him to purchase the leased asset, at the termination of the lease, at a price significantly lower than the expected fair market value of the asset.

3 The life of the lease is greater than 75 percent of the life span of the asset.

4 The present value of the minimum lease payment (MLP) is equal to or greater than 90 percent of the fair market value of leased property.

Lease obligations currently only have to be disclosed as footnotes to the balance sheet. The FASB is keen to enforce these obligations to be included in the core of the balance sheet: leasing footnotes do not reveal the interest portion of future payments.

34

Measuring goodwill

WHAT IS GOODWILL?

Goodwill is usually created when one company buys another and is defined as the difference between the purchase price of an acquired company's assets and their fair market value.

These assets can include such factors as a customer database, distribution channels, contract rights, brand names and trademarks, and other hard-to-evaluate assets.

HOW DO YOU ACCOUNT GOODWILL?

The accounting concept of goodwill has been overhauled several times in recent years. The different approaches used in the past include:

1

AMORTIZATION

Previously, companies were required to amortize goodwill (write if off completely) in equal shares over a period of up to 40 years. Although a company was allowed to keep premiums paid in acquisitions on their books indefinitely, amortization was effectively a noncash charge that reduced the company's reported income.

2 POOLING OF INTEREST

To avoid amortization, companies then chose instead to pool the interests of both companies. This avoided goodwill and therefore avoided any charges to current earnings.

3 IMPAIRMENT

The FASB has in recent years introduced an annual impairment approach that cancels both amortization and pooling of interest. The reason was that FASB didn't think treating goodwill as a wasting asset that deteriorated in value over time, was realistic. Through annual tests, a company now has to determine whether its goodwill is, in fact, permanently declining in value. If the company's current value is lower than what it originally paid for it, then this goodwill must be written down.

The FASB is hoping that the impairment approach will make it easier for nonfinancial experts to spot whether a company has been able to capitalize on a past acquisition, thereby giving it more overall information about its financial health.

principles of accounting

Cost accounting

WHAT IS IT?

Cost accounting describes the process of tracking, recording, and analyzing costs associated with the products or activities of a company. Costs are defined as required resources or time that can include the direct products or material needed for production, in addition to indirect costs such as transport, time, personnel, and other ongoing expenses.

1 STANDARD COSTING

The most common approach, in use for over a century now, is the use of ratios called efficiencies that compare the labor and materials used by a company with the same goods under "standard" conditions. The problem with this approach is that it emphasizes the efficiency of labor that plays a far smaller role in U.S. companies today than it did in the past. Finding a "standard" condition today is also more difficult as competition in manufacturing industries is, in most cases, with companies in developing countries who are working under dramatically different conditions.

2 CONSTRAINTS COST ACCOUNTING

To try to correct some of the problems with standard costing, accountants introduced throughput (or constraints cost), which focuses attention on the relationships between throughput (revenue or income) on one hand and controllable operating expenses and changes in inventory on the other. The onus is on constraints or bottlenecks that prevent the system from producing more throughput.

3 MARGINAL COSTING

Managers use this method to help them make short-term decisions. You simply calculate the total revenue garnered per product and subtract the variable costs to make the product, to leave you with a figure to quantify the contribution made by the product.

Key terms

ACCOUNTING: a company's bookkeeping system that records money coming in and going out of the business.

ACCOUNTING INVENTORY: the process of tracking down all the elements (raw materials, supplies) that make up the production process of most companies that sell products.

ACCRUAL-BASIS ACCOUNTING: accounting method that records revenues and expenses when they are incurred, regardless of the actual period when cash is exchanged (which may be long delayed), for instance sale on credit.

CASH-BASIS ACCOUNTING: accounting method that registers financial events based on cash flows and cash position (i.e., revenue is recognized only when cash is received).

DEPRECIATION: an average or expected view of the decline in value of a company's fixed assets like machinery, equipment, and vehicles. There are several types of depreciation:

STRAIGHT-LINE DEPRECIATION: type of depreciation calculated by taking the purchase cost of the asset and estimating its costs when it is obsolete.

DECLINING-BALANCE DEPRECIATION: type of depreciation that is like straight-line depreciation but estimates that the rate at which the asset loses its value is far higher in the first couple of years than toward the end.

ACTIVITY DEPRECIATION: type of depreciation that focuses on the asset's level of activity.

FASB: Financial Accounting Standards Board; self-regulating body.

FIFO: (first-in, first-out): inventory method that involves taking the first unit that arrived in inventory and transferring it to the cost of the first item sold.

GAAP: generally accepted accounting principles. Companies should conform to these when tracking transactions and preparing financial statements (see pp. 14–15).

IASB: International Accounting Standards Board.

LEASING: renting an asset for a specified period of time in return for a stipulated, and generally periodic, cash payment.

OPERATING LEASE: is when a company records the monthly payment to a leasing company as a rent expense, not as an asset or liability.

CAPITAL LEASE: a lease recorded as both an asset and a liability on the financial statements at the present value of the rental payments.

LIFO (last-in, first-out): inventory method that considers the last unit arriving in inventory and the first one sold.

KEY TERMS

Summary: Accounting basics

1 WHAT IS ACCOUNTING? A company's bookkeeping system that records money coming in and going out of the business.

2 WHY PRACTICE ACCOUNTING? It provides transparency for managers, investors, and creditors. The U.S. Securities and Exchange Commission (SEC) expects all publicly traded companies to follow GAAP (generally accepted accounting principles) and most private companies do.

3 HOW CAN YOU PRACTICE ACCOUNTING?
There are two basic account methods for taxation purposes:

ACCRUAL-BASIS ACCOUNTING.
WHAT IS IT? It records revenues and expenses when they are incurred, regardless of the actual period when cash is exchanged (which may be long delayed).
WHEN DO YOU USE? Use accrual-basis accounting if the company sales are over $10 million, when the company is structured as a corporation, if your business has an inventory, and when your company sells on credit.

PROS: It complies with GAAP, unlike cash-basis accounting.
CONS: It does not indicate the cash inflows and outflows of a company.

CASH-BASIS ACCOUNTING:
WHAT IS IT? It registers financial events based on cash flows and cash position. Revenues and expenses are also called cash receipts and cash payments.
WHEN DO YOU USE? Use cash-basis accounting if you are a small, cash-based business or a small service company, or if you are a sole proprietor or are a business with no inventory.

PROS: Simplicity as books are kept based on the actual flow of cash in and out of the business.
CONS: You are limited by the fact that you can only record actual, not projected, income. You fail to meet two of GAAP's basic principles.

4 WHAT IS COST ACCOUNTING ?
WHAT IS IT? This branch of accounting is the process of tracking, recording, and analyzing costs associated with the products or activities of a company. Costs are defined as required resources or time that can include the direct products or material needed for production and indirect costs such as transport, time, personnel, and other expenses.

HOW DO YOU PRACTICE? There are various ratios called efficiencies such as standard cost accounting that compare the labor and materials used by a company with the same goods under "standard" conditions. There are also activity-based costing (costing by activities) and marginal costing (calculating the total revenue garnered per product).

2

financial concepts
and terminology

financial concepts and terminology

Financial statement

WHAT IS IT?

A financial statement is a written report on the financial condition of a company. Most typically, a financial statement will include:

1. BALANCE SHEET
2. INCOME STATEMENT
3. CASH FLOW STATEMENT

These statements are explained in this chapter.

WHY PREPARE FINANCIAL STATEMENTS?

1

SEC REQUIREMENTS
The Securities and Exchange Commission (SEC) requires publicly traded companies to show financial statements.

2

PRIVATE LENDING REQUIREMENTS
Although private companies are not formally required to produce financial statements, in practice all banks, creditors, and private investors expect to see financial statements that follow generally accepted accounting principles (GAAP, see pp. 14–15).

3 EFFECTIVE MANAGEMENT TOOL

Financial statements enable managers to

- monitor cash flow to identify financing needs early
- measure the effectiveness of the company budget
- check on the company's financial health (indicators such as profitability ratios, liquidity ratios, solvency ratios, and efficiency ratios, see pp. 68–73)
- identify products or services that are selling well or that may need to be discontinued
- spot opportunities to reduce expenditure

WHO PREPARES FINANCIAL STATEMENTS?

Financial statements are usually prepared by certified accountants. In particular, if you are trying to raise finance, this gives lenders an extra measure of security. You can, if your prefer, prepare your own financial statements.

HOW OFTEN DO YOU PRESENT STATEMENTS?

There are no rigid times, but most medium-sized companies find it more useful to have statements prepared every quarter. Smaller businesses may only prepare statements once a year, normally to coincide with the tax year.

financial concepts and terminology

Balance sheet

WHAT IS IT?

The balance sheet is a statement of your company's financial wealth at a single point of time. It's commonly referred to as a snapshot because it gives a clear and instant picture of the business without providing a broader picture of the company's past history or future business.

THE BALANCE SHEET IS BASED ON THE FOLLOWING TERMS:

- ASSETS
- LIABILITIES
- OWNER'S EQUITY

THESE TERMS ARE USED IN THE FOLLOWING FORMULA:

Assets = Liabilities + Owner's equity

1 Assets = all the investments needed by the company to operate the business.

2 Liabilities = all the company's debts, usually taken out to pay for the assets.

3 Owner's equity = the company's net worth once assets are sold and liabilities are paid off.

financial concepts and terminology

Balance sheet continued

WHAT DOES IT LOOK LIKE?

This is a balance sheet of Organics, an organic food production company, for the third quarter.

BALANCE SHEET OF ORGANICS AS OF SEPTEMBER 30

	$	$
CURRENT ASSETS		
Stock	70,000	
Cash	2,000	
Debtors	3,000	75,000
FIXED ASSETS		
Land and buildings	200,000	
Equipment	36,000	
Vehicles	14,000	250,000
INTANGIBLE ASSETS		
Intellectual rights	12,000	
Goodwill	7,000	19,000
INVESTMENTS		
Shares	750	
Insurances	3,500	4,250
TOTAL ASSET VALUE		348,250

CURRENT LIABILITIES	$	$
Bank overdraft	7,400	
Creditors	2,800	
Taxation	3,500	
Proposed dividends	900	14,600
TOTAL ASSETS MINUS		
SHORT-TERM LIABILITIES		333,650
LONG-TERM LIABILITIES		
Loans	4,000	
Mortgage	100,000	104,000
NET ASSET VALUE		229,650

Balance sheet continued

ASSETS

REFERENCE DIAGRAM: EXCERPT FROM BALANCE SHEET

	$	$
CURRENT ASSETS		
Stock	70,000	
Cash	2,000	
Debtors	3,000	75,000
FIXED ASSETS		
Land and buildings	200,000	
Equipment	36,000	
Vehicles	14,000	250,000
INTANGIBLE ASSETS		
Intellectual rights	12,000	
Goodwill	7,000	19,000
INVESTMENTS		
Shares	750	
Insurances	3,500	4,250
TOTAL ASSET VALUE		348,250

ASSETS: WHAT ARE THEY?

1 CURRENT ASSETS
These are the assets in a company that can be converted to cash in one year or less. They include cash, stocks (or inventory such as fruit and vegetables, and finished goods), and debtors.

2 FIXED ASSETS
This refers to the company's assets that cannot be converted to cash within one year, for example, land, equipment, and vehicles.

In addition, the following may be termed assets.

1 INTANGIBLE ASSETS
These are assets that you can't necessarily touch or see. Examples include franchise rights, goodwill, brands, and patents.

2 INVESTMENTS
Investments can be referred to as "other assets." The term covers capital, for instance in shares in other companies or in government securities. Other assets include life insurance and investment property.

Balance sheet continued

LIABILITIES

REFERENCE DIAGRAM: EXCERPT FROM BALANCE SHEET

CURRENT LIABILITIES	$	$
Bank overdraft	7,400	
Creditors	2,800	
Taxation	3,500	
Proposed dividends	900	14,600
Total assets minus short-term liabilities		333,650
LONG-TERM LIABILITIES		
Loans	4,000	
Mortgage	100,000	104,000

LIABILITIES: WHAT ARE THEY?

These describe the group of debts or obligations that the company must pay. They are divided into two principal groups, current liabilities and long-term liabilities:

CURRENT LIABILITES

This refers to debts that have to be paid in the short-term (within 12 months.) It includes:

1 BANK OVERDRAFT

Even though this can be considered a long-term credit, it is technically a temporary facility so it is included as short-term.

2 CREDITORS

These are funds you owe to your suppliers.

Balance sheet continued

CURRENT LIABILITES CONTINUED

3 TAXATION
This can include a number of taxes; see Chapter 6.

4 DIVIDENDS
This refers to the share of the company's profits that are paid to the shareholders, the owners of the company.

5 OTHERS
Other current liabilities not included in this example include notes payable on lines of credit or other short-term loans, current maturities of long-term debt, accounts payable to trade creditors, payroll expenses due to employees for overtime.

LONG-TERM LIABILITIES

These are the obligations of the business that are not due for at least one year. They include:

1 LOANS
These include long-term loans.

2 MORTGAGE
This includes payments for the office buildings and farms payable for several years.

3 STOCKHOLDERS' EQUITY
If the company is listed on the stock exchange, some balance sheets include the total amount invested by the stockholders plus the accumulated profit of the business.

4 OTHERS
This includes bonds payable, and the total of all bonds at the end of the year that are due and payable over a period exceeding one year.

Income statement

WHAT IS IT?

While the balance sheet is a financial snapshot, an income statement is a summary of your company's flow of transactions during the period between balance sheets. This period can be a financial quarter or at the end of the fiscal year.

The main purpose of the income statement is to find out how much profit (or loss) the company has made. For this reason, an income statement is also commonly known as a profit and loss statement, or profit and loss account.

WHAT DOES IT LOOK LIKE?

This is the income statement of Organics for one year.

ORGANICS INCOME STATEMENT FOR YEAR ENDING DECEMBER 31

	$	$
SALES		950,000
Less COST OF GOODS SOLD		
Materials	220,000	
Farm	80,000	
Direct labor	190,000	490,000
GROSS PROFIT		460,000
Less OVERHEADS		
Administration	120,000	
Delivery	80,000	
Sales and advertising	20,000	
Professional fees	8,000	228,000
TRADING PROFIT		232,000
Interest paid	10,000	
PRE-TAX PROFITS		222,000
Taxation	14,000	
AFTER-TAX PROFITS		208,000
Interim dividend (paid)	8,000	
Final dividend (proposed)	12,000	
NET PROFIT		188,000

Income statement continued

REFERENCE DIAGRAM: EXCERPT FROM INCOME STATEMENT

	$	$
SALES		950,000
Less COST OF GOODS SOLD		
Materials	220,000	
Farm expenses	80,000	
Direct labor	190,000	490,000

SALES:
This figures refers to the total sales of Organics in one fiscal year.

COSTS OF GOODS SOLD refers to costs directly associated with making the products.

MATERIALS covers the cost of raw materials that Organics has to produce in its farms or buy from suppliers and the cost of manufacturing dried products from these raw materials.

FARM EXPENSES are the costs of running the farms.

DIRECT LABOR refers to wages of the workers directly involved with production.

REFERENCE DIAGRAM: EXCERPT FROM INCOME STATEMENT

	$	$
GROSS PROFIT		460,000
Less OVERHEADS		
Administration	120,000	
Delivery	80,000	
Sales and advertising	20,000	
Professional fees	8,000	228,000

GROSS PROFITS:
Sales—cost of goods sold. From this amount you have to deduct:

OVERHEADS are all costs the company incurs that don't include direct costs above. They include:

ADMINISTRATION (the salaries of administrative staff), stationery, and accountancy;

DELIVERY (any costs involved in transporting the goods to customers and between facilities);

SALES AND ADVERTISING (any promotions for the shop or the products);

PROFESSIONAL FEES (covering the use of suppliers such as solicitors and accountants).

Income statement continued

REFERENCE DIAGRAM: EXCERPT FROM INCOME STATEMENT

	$	$
TRADING PROFIT		232,000
Interest paid	10,000	
PRE-TAX PROFITS		222,000
Taxation	14,000	
AFTER-TAX PROFITS		208,000
Interim dividend (paid)	8,000	
Final dividend (proposed)	12,000	
NET PROFIT		188,000

1 TRADING PROFIT is also known as OPERATING PROFIT (before interest and tax are deducted).

2 INTEREST refers to interest incurred on all loans.

3 PRE-TAX PROFITS are the trading profit minus the interest paid.

4 AFTER-TAX PROFITS are the trading profit (also known as the "bottom line" earnings of a company). They are the pre-tax profits minus the interest paid and minus taxation.

5 DIVIDENDS are the amount of cash paid out to shareholders in a public company. The money can be invested in future business or invested back into the company.

financial concepts and terminology

Cash flow statement

WHAT IS A CASH FLOW STATEMENT?

A cash flow statement is a financial report that shows incoming and outgoing money during a particular period.

WHAT DOES A CASH FLOW STATEMENT LOOK LIKE?

ORGANICS CASH FLOW STATEMENT FOR ONE YEAR

	$
Net income	208,000
Operating assets and liabilities	
Accounts receivable	-126,000
Inventory	55,000
Prepaid insurance	-5,000
Other current assets	10,000
Accounts payable	20,000
Wages payable	-70,000
Interest payable	-2,000
Income taxes payable	-39,000
Accrued expenses	-34,000
Total changes in operating assets and liabilities	(-191,000)
Cash flow from operations	**17,000**

CONTINUED

	$
Investing activities	
Land	80,000
Buildings	100,000
Equipment	35,000
Vehicles	20,000
Capital expenditures	-200,000
Cash flow from investing activities	**35,000**
Financing activities	
Bonds payable	-1,000
Deferred income taxes	-2,000
Repayment of loans	-2,500
Issue of shares	-3,000
Dividends	-4,000
Long-term loans	130,000
Cash flow from financing activities	**117,500**
Increase in cash during year	**169,500**

Cash flow statement continued

CASH FLOW STATEMENT EXPLAINED

REFERENCE DIAGRAM: EXCERPT FROM CASH FLOW STATEMENT

	$
Operating assets and liabilities	
Accounts receivable	126,000
Inventory	55,000
Prepaid insurance	-5,000
Other current assets	10,000
Accounts payable	20,000
Wages payable	-70,000
Interest payable	-2,000
Income taxes payable	-39,000
Accrued expenses	34,000
Total changes in operating assets and liabilities	(-191,000)
Cash flow from operations	**17,000**

OPERATING ACTIVITIES. The costs of operations and delayed payments means that cash flow from operations is a modest $17,000

	$
Investing activities	
Land	80,000
Buildings	100,000
Equipment	35,000
Vehicles	20,000
Capital expenditures	-200,000
Cash flow from investing activities	**35,000**

INVESTING ACTIVITIES. Organics has sold part of its investments (land and equipment) to cover capital expenditure.

Cash flow statement continued

	$
Financing activities	
Bonds payable	-1,000
Deferred income taxes	-2,000
Repayment of loans	-2,500
Issue of shares	-3,000
Dividends	-4,000
Long-term loans	130,000
Cash flow from financing activities	117,500
Increase in cash during year	169,500

FINANCING ACTIVITIES

The increase in cash during the year is $169,500. This is less than the company's net income of $208,000.

This reveals that the company's net income or earnings are referred to as "moderate" to "low" quality because the reported net income is not turning into sufficient cash.

Furthermore, Organics has had to take a major loan of $130,000 to make up for the modest cash flow from its operating and investing activities.

Potential investors would want further reassurances that the company could increase net income before considering advancing funds.

Understanding the numbers

To assess the financial health of a company, managers, analysts, and investors use more than numbers extracted from the financial statements. They need to put figures like net profits or overall sales into context. Ratios are one of the most common methods to compare your company with other companies, both in the same sector and with companies of the same size but in a different industry.

There are three main ratios commonly used, all of which are expressed as a percentage. They can all be established from financial statements.

1 LIQUIDITY RATIOS

These are the most commonly used ratios since they tell a buyer or investor quickly whether the company is able to generate enough cash to pay its outstanding bills. They come in two forms:

CURRENT RATIO: looks at the company's working capital. You use the format $x:y$, with x standing for the amount of current assets and y the amount of current liabilities. Traditional lenders often require a current ratio of 2:1 for any significant loans. Merely paying off some current liabilities can improve your current ratio.
For example, Organics' current assets total $75,000 and current liabilities are $14,600 which is a current ratio of 5:1, an unusually healthy ratio.

QUICK RATIO (also known as acid-test): is similar to the current ratio but doesn't include inventory in current assets. The reason is that inventory can be turned to cash only through sales, so the quick ratio gives you a more accurate picture of a company's ability to meet its short-term obligations.

In the case of Organics, subtracting inventory from the equation creates a radical difference as the stock is worth $70,000, leaving only $5,000 worth of assets. The ratio would now be totally reversed at 1:2.5. A good quick ratio is 1:1. One solution is for Organics to convert inventory to cash or accounts receivable.

REFERENCE DIAGRAM: EXCERPT FROM BALANCE SHEET OF ORGANICS
AS OF SEPTEMBER 30

	$	$
CURRENT ASSETS		
Stock	70,000	
Cash	2,000	
Debtors	3,000	75,000
CURRENT LIABILITIES		
Bank overdraft	7,400	
Creditors	2,800	
Taxation	3,500	
Proposed dividends	900	14,600

Understanding the numbers continued

2 PROFITABILITY RATIOS
The following ratios best reveal the performance and growth potential of your company

GROSS PROFIT MARGIN RATIO

This is calculated by taking your gross profits and dividing them by your sales and then multiplying by 100 to give a percentage.

In the case of Organics:
Gross profits = $460,000
Sales = $950,000
$460,000 ÷ $950,000 =
0.48 x 100 = 48 percent

Obviously, the higher the percentage, the better the margin. The real test for the company is to compare the margin across a number of years. If the margin declines over time, selling prices may be too low or production costs may be too high.

OPERATING PROFIT PERCENTAGE

This ratio is aimed at demonstrating how much money the company is making on its primary business.

The formula is:
Operating (or trading) income divided by sales, multiplied by 100 to give a percentage.

In Organics' case:
Operating income = $232,000
Sales = $950,000
$232,000 ÷ $950,000 =
0.244 x 100 = 24.4 percent

This ratio is designed to give you an accurate idea of how much money you're making on your primary business operations. It shows the percentage of each sales dollar remaining after all normal costs of operations have been made.

NET PROFIT MARGIN

This margin shows how much of each sales dollar is available to the company at any given point, since it takes into account all expenses including income taxes and interest.

The formula is:
Net income divided by sales multiplied by 100 to give a percentage.

In Organics' case:
Net income = $208,000
Sales = $950,00
$208,000 ÷ $950,000 =
0.218 x 100 = 21.8 percent

To assess whether this is a positive rate, you have to compare with the company's performance over time and also with other companies in the same sector.

Understanding the numbers continued

3 SOLVENCY RATIOS

One of many ratios used to measure a company's ability to meet long-term obligations (its solvency) is a debt ratio. This demonstrates the proportion of the company's assets that have been financed by debt.

The formula of debt ratio is: Total liabilities divided by total assets, multiplied by 100 to create a percentage.
In Organics' case:

Total liabilities = $118,600
Total assets = $348, 250
$118,600 ÷ $348,250 = 0.34 x 100 = 34 percent

A low debt ratio is safer than a high debt ratio because a company with fewer liabilities has fewer payments going out than a company with a high debt ratio.

REFERENCE DIAGRAM: EXCERPT FROM BALANCE SHEET OF ORGANICS AS OF SEPTEMBER 30

CURRENT ASSETS	$	$
Stock	70,000	
Cash	2,000	
Debtors	3,000	75,000

	$	$
FIXED ASSETS		
Land and buildings	200,000	
Equipment	36,000	
Vehicles	14,000	250,000
INTANGIBLE ASSETS		
Intellectual rights	12,000	
Goodwill	7,000	19,000
INVESTMENTS		
Shares	750	
Insurances	3,500	4,250
TOTAL ASSET VALUE		348,250
CURRENT LIABILITIES		
Bank overdraft	7,400	
Creditors	2,800	
Taxation	3,500	
Proposed dividends	900	14,600
Total assets less short-term liabilities		333,650
LONG-TERM LIABILITIES		
Loans	4,000	
Mortgage	100,000	104,000
NET ASSET VALUE		229,650

Key terms

ASSETS: all the company's investments needed to operate the company. They include:

  BUSINESS ASSETS: a company's overall resources.
  CURRENT ASSETS: assets in a company that can be converted to cash in one year or less including bank drafts, checks, currency, deposit account, finished goods, inventory, money orders, and stocks.
  FIXED ASSETS: assets that cannot be converted to cash within one year like land, equipment, and vehicles.
  INTANGIBLE ASSETS: nonphysical assets like franchise rights, goodwill, brands, patents, and many other items.

BALANCE SHEET: a statement of a company's financial wealth at a single point of time, often described as a snapshot.

CASH FLOW STATEMENT: a financial report showing incoming and outgoing money during a particular period, either on a monthly, quarterly, or annual basis.

DIVIDENDS: share of the company's profits paid to the shareholders, the owners of the company.

FINANCIAL STATEMENT: a written report on the financial condition of a company.

INCOME STATEMENT: summary of a company's flow of transactions during the period (a financial quarter or end of fiscal year) between balance sheets.

INVESTMENT: capital placed outside the company like shares in other companies or in government securities, life insurance, and long-term investment property.

LIABILITIES: group of debts or obligations that a company takes out to pay for the assets.

CURRENT LIABILITIES: debts that have to be paid in the short-term (within 12 months) including bank overdraft, taxation, dividends, notes payable on lines of credit or other short-term loans, current maturities of long-term debt, accounts payable to trade creditors, payroll expenses due to employees for overtime.

LONG-TERM LIABILITIES: obligations of the business that are not due for at least one year like loans, mortgages, stockholders equity, and bonds.

OWNER'S EQUITY: the company's net worth after assets are sold and liabilities paid off.

KEY TERMS

Summary: Financial statements

1
WHY HAVE A FINANCIAL STATEMENT?
All companies are required by the SEC to prepare
financial statements.

2
WHAT DOES A FINANCIAL STATEMENT CONSIST OF?

BALANCE SHEET: A snapshot of assets, liabilities, and owner's equity.

INCOME STATEMENT: A summary of flow of transactions during the
period between balance sheets to find out how much profit (or
losses) the company has made.

CASH FLOW STATEMENT: A financial report that shows incoming and
outgoing money during a particular period, either on a monthly,
quarterly, or annual basis.

3
WHO PREPARES A FINANCIAL STATEMENT?
Typically, certified accountants prepare a financial statement, but
managers can also prepare them.

4 HOW OFTEN DO YOU PREPARE A FINANCIAL STATEMENT?
There are no rigid times but most usefully, every quarter.

5 HOW DO YOU ASSESS A FINANCIAL STATEMENT?
You need to put figures like net profits or overall sales into context.
The most common ways are by using ratios, usually expressed as a
percentage. They include:

LIQUIDITY RATIOS: They tell a buyer or investor quickly whether the
company is able to generate enough cash to pay its outstanding bills.

PROFITABILITY RATIOS: They reveal the performance and growth
potential of your company.

SOLVENCY RATIOS: They measure a company's ability to meet long-
term obligations and demonstrate the proportion of the company's
assets that have been financed by debt.

KEY QUESTIONS

financing daily operations

Why budget?

The key to successful financing of daily operations is to budget.
These are some of the key benefits of a well-planned budget:

1 ANTICIPATE PROBLEMS
The process of budgeting forces you to anticipate and prevent
problems. It demands that you estimate how much capital
you are going to need for your daily operations and how you
will meet these financial obligations without facing a cash
flow crisis.

2 PERSUADE BACKERS
With a budget that anticipates potential bottlenecks in your
operations and delays in cash flows, you will be in a better
position to make a case for a loan from your bank or
investment fund.

3 MEASURE RESULTS
A budget or plan helps you keep score: effectively you are meeting your objectives because you have a concrete list of landmarks or targets against which you can measure results.

4 IDENTIFY PROBLEMS
Budgets try to create the most ideal scenario for your business to follow, but they can also throw up any potential challenges or obstacles that you might otherwise have ignored in your pursuit of preferred results.

Why budget? continued

5 IMPROVE DECISION MAKING
When you lay out a template of what the company can achieve and how much it will cost, you are in a better position to make some tricky decisions such as dropping a favorite project because the figures won't add up or to pursue a strategy that you had written off initially.

6 MOTIVATE STAFF
A budget helps staff to understand what direction the company is going and the parameters in which it is working. Workers can follow targets, such as sales figures or number of new customers recruited, and measure how well they are performing.

7 SAVE TIME
While many managers feel that the research and paperwork involved in preparing a budget can cause unnecessary delays to the core operations of the business, the opposite is in fact true. Lack of planning will inevitably lead to stalled projects while directors grapple with problems that could have been anticipated at an earlier stage.

8 CREATE STRATEGY
You may have a clear idea of what the business needs to achieve in the short term, but you may have overlooked how the company and the sector you are working in may change in 12 months' time. A budget can help develop a picture of the future and force you to implement relevant strategies to cope with any adverse conditions.

financing daily operations

What is a budget?

A budget is a tool for converting plans into reality. It covers the process of defining objectives; forecasting expectations of sales, profits, and expenses of every sort; deciding what actions will best help the company achieve these targets; determining how much money will be needed to support these actions; and, finally, providing a way to monitor whether the actions chosen are the most appropriate at the current time, or whether they need to be modified in some way.

FEATURES OF A BUDGET
A budget should include the following components to be effective:

1 Clearly defined objectives, both short- and long-term.

2 Estimates of revenue amounts.

3 An analysis of revenue payments: how far do they lag behind payment of expenses?

4 Estimates of expense amounts and timing of expense payments.

5 A list of ongoing direct and indirect costs.

6 A cash budget to predict cash flow over time.

7 Procedures to monitor the progress of the budget.

What is a budget? continued

TIMING OF A BUDGET

1 There are no fixed time periods a budget should cover. The longest-range budgets can cover a period of between three and five years, although the most typical period is one year, to coincide with the company's financial year. This is called a fixed budget.

2 Even an annual budget is typically split into quarterly or monthly statements to make the process more manageable and easier to follow. A fixed budget that is regularly updated to keep up with rapid changes in the company's particular sector is sometimes called a rolling budget.

3 Some businesses budget on a 1–4 week cycle, but these are most effective when they work within a longer time framework.

4 For a one-year cycle, it is best to set the next budget at least three months before the end of the current budget. For a shorter-term budget (one month, for instance), the process should have started at least by the third week of the current budget.

Defining objectives

Budgets are made primarily to help meet objectives. As a result, the type of budget you devise will vary considerably depending on the ultimate purpose of the plan. The following steps will help you define your objectives:

1

UNDERSTAND YOUR COMPANY
Identifying your company's Strengths, Weaknesses, Opportunities, and Threats (a popular technique known as SWOT) can help you amass valuable facts that will help you identify necessary action to take:
STRENGTHS: What advantages does your company have over rivals?
WEAKNESSES: Where is the company underperforming and what are competitors doing better and why?
OPPORTUNITIES: Where are the biggest chances for growth?
THREATS: What are the biggest obstacles facing you: for example, competition, or shortage of investment capital?

2

LISTEN TO COMPANY SECTIONS
If you are a small company, it will be easier for you to identify the core strengths, weaknesses, opportunities, and threats but in a larger company, these may vary significantly. You need to gather information from different departments to ensure their needs are met by the budget. For instance, marketing and advertising may be understaffed, and this could negatively affect overall sales, no matter how much time you've put into improving the core product.

3 SUMMARIZE CORE AIMS

Summaries of the core objectives of the company and the different departments, or mission statements, could include
- "We are trying to increase revenue."
- "We want to raise market share by xx."
- "We need to focus on cutting costs."
- "We need to research new product lines."

4 SET FINANCIAL TARGETS

Make sure you have taken into account the financial targets of every department, including
- marketing and advertising
- purchasing/inventory
- personnel
- administration
- finance department
- sales
- customer service

financing daily operations

Start-up objectives

For start-ups, as well as following the steps outlined on pp. 86–87, it may be useful to try to answer the following set of questions to help you make some reasonable assumptions about your business and its early days of operating and trading:

1 How many products/services do you expect to sell in the first year?

2 Can you predict a rate of sales growth for the next three years?

3 How will you price your products/services?

4 What will be the cost of producing your product/service?

5 What will your operating expenses be?

6 How many employees do you intend to hire and how much will you pay them?

7 Have you established whether your business will be a proprietorship, a partnership, or a corporation? The tax consequences of each form will vary considerably (see pp. 190–203).

8 Will you be leasing/renting/buying an office? What will the costs be?

9 How much finance will you need to raise? What is the interest rate on funds that you are borrowing?

10 Will you sell on credit? Have you established what payment terms you will get from suppliers and what you will offer customers?

Gathering information

Once you have identified your objectives, you need to turn to the important process of gathering key information to enable you to create the budget.

ESTIMATING SALES AND REVENUE

As sales of products and services are the lifeblood of most companies, you will inevitably start with a projection of sales and revenue. This can be a tricky process because it involves guessing the future, but there are certain actions you can take to make a forecast easier. Assume that your company is a furniture shop.

1 USE PAST SALES
Unless you are a start-up, looking at last year's figures is a good place to start as it is based on real figures. Imagine you are looking at the last quarter of the year—October to December sales. It is worth noting some of the dangers to this approach, also known as incremental budgeting, which means using historical figures. You can't assume that the sales figures of the same period the previous year will naturally rise by a certain percentage without studying the sales patterns in the interim period. Only if there has been a consistently steady rise throughout the year, is it safe to predict further growth.

2 DISTINGUISH BETWEEN PRODUCTS
To more accurately assess last year's sales figures, it is useful
to break down overall sales by product to see if there is some
trend in sales. Were the best-selling products for the last
quarter—sofas, for example—also popular goods throughout
the rest of the year or can you detect a seasonal pattern?

3 LOOK AT THE COMPETITION
Are rival furniture companies in the area selling well? Is the
sector positive because there is a general property boom, or can
you predict a slowdown in the market due to external factors?

4 ASK SUPPLIERS
Suppliers may also give you an indication of trends. For example, a fabric supplier may suggest that traditional upholstered sofas are losing ground to models upholstered in leather or other materials.

5 READ SECTOR REPORTS
Sector reports compiled by research companies can provide information on projected sales based on area or nationwide sales figures.

6 STUDY INNOVATIVE PRODUCTS
Are you planning to launch a new line that you expect to sell particularly well, at least when it is new? Does this have to be factored into estimates?

7 MONITOR CASH FLOW

Once you have established revenue types and revenue amounts, it is important to predict a pattern of payments. Typically, how long do customers take to pay for the products? How much is sold on credit? Can you extrapolate from the accounting department some sort of payment pattern from the quarter of the previous year and also throughout the rest of the year? Will you have to take on additional borrowing to finance the purchase of new product lines to prevent cash flow problems?

Gathering information continued

ESTIMATING EXPENDITURE

The next part of your budget should include all the costs of operation involved in producing and delivering the product or service to customers. These are factors that need to be considered:

1

DEFINE EXPENDITURE TYPES

There are four main types of costs that a company will typically incur:

1. CAPITAL COSTS: These include all tangible assets that a company may have acquired (as a one-time purchase) and include a company office, office machinery, any equipment or machinery if you are a manufacturer, and nontangible assets like brands and goodwill—see Chapter 1.
2. SPECIFIC PRODUCT COSTS: These refer to all costs that are driven by particular products such as the labor and raw materials needed to make a line of sofas, the transportation of the sofas from the warehouse, and the after-sales support.
3. ONGOING COSTS: These are regular costs that most companies have to pay, such as electricity and telecommunications, lease or rent of an office, stationery, wages for full-time employees, and advertising.
4. START-UP COSTS: These refer to specific purchases made by start-ups such as pre-launch literature and license fees.

2 DEFINE EXPENDITURE TIMING

As with payment of invoices and receipts, it is just as important to establish the exact timings of payments you must make to help you anticipate any cash flow problems.

CHECK WITH DEPARTMENTS about the dates they have to pay for specific services. Can they make any adjustments such as paying creditors quarterly rather than monthly? Are there any unexpected, one-time costs that they haven't written down? Which payments can be delayed and which ones will incur most interest? Was an analysis made on last year's overall expenditure? Did the company detect areas where potential savings could be made and, if so, have these savings been factored in this year's budget?

3 ESTIMATE PROFITS/LOSS

The next part of your budget is the total profit or loss from operations, which you will be able to calculate from the list of predicted costs and expenses. As in the previous estimates, try to define a general profit trend.

Gathering information continued

CHALLENGING THE FIGURES

At this stage, you may feel confident about stating some figures (more typically expenditure because these are easier to predict) and more nervous about sales and profit figures, mainly because these are subject to a number of variables such as the action of competitors or changes in the economy that you have not foreseen.

The following approaches may be helpful in allowing you to challenge the figures that you have initially compiled.

1 **"WHAT-IF" SCENARIOS**
You might want to change the figures by working on the assumption that the final result is not as favorable to the company as you had hoped. By working on a more pessimistic scenario, you are laying out contingency plans. You can try adding, for instance, 10 percent to some of the expenses while subtracing 10 percent from some revenues. To avoid becoming too negative, you could include two sets of figures, underlying which you place your initial set of projected figures.

2 ZERO-BASED BUDGETING

Zero-based budgeting describes the process where a company decides on what it wants to achieve, how this can be achieved, and what resources it needs to implement the result. Also known as bottom-down budgeting, this method runs contrary to the more common practice used by many companies to make budgetary decisions based on past performance.

ADVANTAGES
■ It doesn't rely on previous years' figures, which could be wrong.
■ It prevents managers from missing any previous cost changes.
■ It forces managers to reassess a company's needs from scratch and not to rely on previous budget sizes, which may be unnecessarily large.

DISADVANTAGES
■ Zero-based budgeting takes longer and is more costly.
■ It may encourage unnecessary frugality that has negative repercussions on staff morale.
■ It may work for certain departments and in certain years but can be cumbersome if carried out regularly.

3 ACTIVITY-BASED COSTING

Although a more costly and time-consuming approach, activity-based costing involves costing different activities by looking at timesheets and results. This method can work for result-driven activities but is less successful when boosting sales is not the prime activity.

Creating a cash budget

Planning for a final (commonly called master) budget will be incomplete without a cash budget. This will show how money will be moved to and from the business bank account to make it possible to finance the company's activities.

BENEFITS

1

PLANNING TOOL

A cash budget shows the cash effect of all plans made in the budget. If the cash flow is negative, the company knows it either has to put more pressure on debtors or seek further sources of finance. For instance, disbursements are lumped together, and you need to spread your payments to creditors more evenly throughout the year. This will lower bank credit and interest costs.

2

WARNING SIGNAL

A cash budget may also give management a sign of the potential problems that could emerge and gives them time to take action to avoid such problems.

CASH BUDGET SAMPLE

This is an example of what a simple cash flow forecast looks like. It covers the three month period (October-December) for the furniture store considered on pp. 92–95.

PROFIT AND LOSS ACCOUNT		TIMING OF CASH FLOW	ACTUAL CASH RECEIPTS		
				MONTH	
PRODUCT	$		OCT	NOV	DEC
Sales	+45,000	Two months credit	+3,000	+2,000	+2,200
Purchases (supp.)	-28,000	Three months credit	-1,500	-1,500	-1,500
Wages	-3,000	Immediate	-1,000	-1,000	-1,000
Rent	-2,000	One month in advance	-2,000	-2,000	-2,000
Electricity	-900	One month credit	-900	-900	-900
Insurance	-120	Six months in advance	0	0	0
Advertising	-750	Three months credit	-750	-750	-750
Profit	**+11,230**	**Monthly cash flow**	**-1,165**	**-2,665**	**-2,465**
(REVENUE MINUS EXPENDITURE)					

Creating a cash budget continued

NOTES ON SAMPLE

1

The forecast shows that even though the company enjoys a healthy monthly profit of $11,230—thanks largely to robust sales—the cash flow is negative every month due to late payments of invoices. The company knows it must take steps to obtain financing to cover the shortfall or improve the speed with which invoices are paid.

2

This chart doesn't include any interest payments on loans or overdrafts, which will impinge more negatively on the monthly cash flow. It also does not factor in how long stock remains in store. The longer the time gap between the company buying stock and shipping it out again, the greater the impact on overall profits.

3 The timing of cash receipts and payments may not coincide with the recording of profit and loss account transactions. For instance, the company may have made a significant sales order, but late payment of the receipt means that the income won't be available for another three months. The company still has to proceed with new financing. Money to fund this type of transaction is usually not difficult to secure, but interest payments need to be taken into account.

Monitoring the budget

After a budget has been written and approved, the task of monitoring the budget begins. Inevitably, actual events will produce results that vary from the budget. These are recommended steps to monitor the results.

1

SET A TIME PERIOD

With an annual budget, you will have to wait a couple of months after the end of the year. However, most budgets allow for quarterly, if not monthly, observations based on monthly projections.

2

REGISTER ACTUAL RESULTS

The first step is to write down the results achieved by the company and compare them with projections. Any discrepancies are typically called variances. When the variances are over 10 percent, it is worth looking into the reasons.

3

CATEGORIZE VARIANCES

It is easier to assess the variances that concern you by categorizing them into price, volume, and timing.

4 ANALYZE VARIANCES
With each variance, ask what could have led to the miscalculation. The causes are usually budget errors, the result of poor preparation, or changes that result from external factors such as economic change.

5 TAKE CAUTIOUS ACTION
Sometimes it's better not to take swift action. Blaming staff for not forecasting an event, when in reality they had few ways of predicting a result, can damage morale. Be cautious. If you can make amends, look at the expense and find out if there are ways of reducing overhead.

6 REVIEW TARGETS
Some variances may be the result of overly optimistic revenue projections. Were the sales targets unattainable? Study performance of competitors and analyze whether targets were realistic.

7 REVIEW PROCESS
You should review the way the budget was put together. Were the objectives set by top management in a top-down fashion? Were middle and lower ranking directors encouraged to provide their opinions on the company goals?

Key terms

AMORTIZATION: the act of writing off goodwill completely.

BUDGET: the process of defining objectives; forecasting expectations of sales, profits, and expenses of every sort; deciding what actions will best help the company achieve these targets; determining how much money will be needed to support these actions; and, finally, providing a way to monitor that the actions chosen are appropriate or whether they need to be modified.

GOODWILL: the difference between the purchase price of an acquired company's assets and its fair market value.

COST ACCOUNTING: the process of tracking, recording, and analyzing costs associated with the products or activities of a company.

COSTS:
CAPITAL COSTS: all tangible assets that a company may have acquired (as a one-time purchase), including a company office, office machinery, any equipment or machinery, and nontangible assets like brands, patents, and goodwill.

ONGOING COSTS: regular costs that most companies have to pay such as electricity and telecommunications, lease or rent of an office, stationery, wages for full-time employees, and advertising.

SPECIFIC PRODUCT COSTS: all costs that are driven by particular products such as the labor and raw materials needed to make products.

START-UP COSTS: specific purchases made by start-ups such as pre-launch literature and license fees.

COSTING:
ACTIVITY-BASED COSTING: costing by activities that define any actions that a company takes regularly as part of its day-to-day operations.

MARGINAL COSTING: costing by calculating the total revenue garnered per product and subtracting the variable costs to make the product.

STANDARD COSTING: a standard approach to costing that uses ratios called efficiencies that compare the labor and materials used by a company with the same goods under "standard" conditions.

SWOT: Strengths, Weaknesses, Opportunities, and Threats (a popular technique used by a company to help make a decision).

ZERO-BASED BUDGETING: the process whereby a company decides what target it wants to achieve, how this can be achieved, and what resources it needs to implement the result; also known as bottom-down budgeting.

KEY TERMS

Key questions: Budgets

1

WHY BUDGET?
Budgeting forces companies to anticipate and prevent problems, create strategy, measure results, motivate staff, and save time.

2

WHAT IS IT?
A budget covers the process of defining objectives; forecasting expectations of sales, profits, and expenses of every sort; deciding what actions will best help the company achieve these targets; deciding how much money will be needed to support these actions; and finally, providing a way to monitor whether the actions chosen are appropriate or whether they need to be modified.

3

WHEN SHOULD A BUDGET BE CREATED?
There are no fixed time periods a budget should cover. The longest range budgets can cover a period of between three and five years. A more typical period is one year, to coincide with the company's financial year.

4 HOW SHOULD A BUDGET BE CREATED?

DEFINE OBJECTIVES by understanding your company, listening to company sections, summarizing core aims, setting financial targets, and defining start-up objectives.

GATHER INFORMATION by estimating sales and revenue, estimating expenditure, estimating profits/loss, and challenging the figures.

CREATE A CASH BUDGET. No final (or master) budget can be complete without a cash budget that will show how money will be moved to and from the business bank account.

5 HOW SHOULD A BUDGET BE MONITORED?

SET A TIME PERIOD. Although some companies operate on an annual budget, most allow for quarterly, if not monthly, observations.

REGISTER ACTUAL RESULTS. Write down the results achieved by the company and compare them with projections.

CATEGORIZE VARIANCES. Divide into price, volume, and timing.

ANALYZE VARIANCES. Ask yourself in each of the categories, what could have led to the miscalculation.

REVIEW PROCESS. Finally, review the way the budget was put together. It may be that the objectives were unrealistic or not defined specifically enough.

KEY QUESTIONS

4

financing growth

Debt vs. equity financing

This chapter deals with a host of financial sources a company can turn to, whether it is a start-up or an established company that is seeking to expand. It begins by laying out two fundamental choices facing any company that is seeking finance: debt vs. equity.

DEBT FINANCING

WHAT IS IT?

Debt financing describes the borrowing of money. The loan usually accumulates interest at a future date unless you borrow from a relative or business colleague at no interest.

ADVANTAGES

1 The company doesn't sacrifice any ownership interests.

2 The interest on the loan is tax deductible.

3 The cost of financing the debt is a relatively fixed expense.

DISADVANTAGES

1 You accumulate interest on the repayments. This varies from reasonable to high depending on conditions, for instance if the interest rate fluctuates. Too many loans can be damaging during a business downturn.

2 Too much debt financing can harm your credit rating and your success in borrowing money in the future.

3 Excess debt makes your business look risky and a dangerous investment, a negative point if you want to eventually go down the "equity finance" route.

Debt vs. equity financing continued

SOURCES OF DEBT FINANCING
For more detail, see pp. 124–157 on business life cycles.

1 Banks

2 Savings and loans/commercial finance companies

3 Small Business Administration (SBA)

4 Leasing

5 Asset-based financing

6 Trade credit

Equity financing

WHAT IS IT?

Equity financing is a term that describes an exchange of money or capital in return for a share of business ownership. This involves selling the future benefits and profits of your business to investors. Sometimes, the company can inject equity from its profits or from any savings.

ADVANTAGES

1 This form of financing allows you to obtain funds without incurring debt or having to repay a specific amount of money at any particular time.

2 Your chances of future cash borrowing are boosted if traditional lenders can see that you have a reasonable cushion available for repayment of a debt in the case of a default. An acceptable debt-to-equity ratio is considered to be between 1:2 and 1:1.

DISADVANTAGES

1 By selling a percentage of the ownership in your business, you may sacrifice some of your autonomy and management rights. This may be less of a problem if you are not necessarily interested in maintaining the business indefinitely and intend to sell your interests for a fair profit in the short term.

2 Finding investors who are willing to buy into your business takes time, effort, and particular powers of persuasion.

3 Too much equity financing can indicate that you aren't using your capital productively enough as leverage for obtaining cash advances.

Equity financing continued

WHO PROVIDES EQUITY FINANCING?

See also business life cycles, pp. 124–157.

1 Angel investors

2 Venture capitalists

3 Small business investment companies (SBICs), the government's venture capital business

4 Initial public offerings (IPOs)

5 Limited private offerings of ownership interests

6 Employee stock ownership plans (ESOPs)

7 Franchising

8 Money markets (domestic and international)

Financing the business cycle

Most companies will access both debt and equity financing, in different combinations, during the course of a business life cycle. This section aims to point out the myriad choices within these two basic types of financing by linking them with the main stages of the business life cycle.

For the purposes of clarity, this section will refer to four main stages of the business life cycle. These are

1 Seed

2 Start-up

3 Growth

4 Maturity

Financing the business cycle continued

IT IS IMPORTANT TO REMEMBER THAT

1 Companies develop in similar stages to human beings. The strategies adopted by parents in the early years of a child's life aren't going to be necessarily appropriate during the teenage years. Successful companies will be able to understand where their business fits on their life cycle, foresee upcoming challenges, and make better decisions.

2 Not all companies will follow the four stages of the business life cycle in the same way. Some businesses will catapult up the ladder from start-up to maturity, especially in the technological sector, while others in more traditional sectors will take a more cautious route and avoid expansion in the early years. Many companies will grow steadily until they hit a major setback that stalls their growth for longer than initial assessments suggested.

Amazon.com, the Nasdaq-quoted electronic commerce company, will be used in the following examination as a prime example of a company that has experienced the four stages of a business life cycle in an unusually short time. It can be argued that a company that was only launched in 1994 can hardly have reached maturity. But in the topsy-turvy dot.com world, a decade of success, let alone survival, is a long time. Certainly, as one of the first companies to sell goods over the Internet, Amazon is fairly unique in its meteoric rise. Yet it can prove illustrative of the many financial resources available to much smaller companies with less global pretensions.

Financing the seed stage

WHAT IS IT?

The seed stage of your business life cycle is when your business is just a thought or an idea. This is the very birth or conception of a new company.

THE CHALLENGE

Most seed stage companies are either struggling to enter an already crowded market with a new proposition or are breaking new territory completely by pursuing a niche opportunity.

The now legendary story goes that Amazon.com's founder, Jeff Bezos, conceived the idea of an online bookstore while he was on a car journey to Seattle with his wife. While she drove, he typed the business plan on a laptop.

SOURCES OF FINANCE

Few, if any, new companies are ever started with formal venture capital or funding from commercial banks. Such institutions need to see some evidence of long-term collateralized loans for asset acquisitions. At this early stage, the typical entrepreneur has to make the most of his persuasive powers to attract funds from people closest to him, who know him well enough to take a risk on potential success.

1

FAMILY/FRIENDS

These are the most likely candidates to back a horse who has ideas, passion, and vision but who has so far won few races. If you're lucky, relatives can invest between $5,000 and $20,000 in this first preliminary round of fund raising.

In the case of Bezos, he was already a young star in his field (hedge funds) in New York and had some track record in the working world. Allegedly, his father, a former engineer with oil company ExxonMobil, was in the position to lend him $300,000. It is possible that in exchange for these unsecured loans, you will have to provide family investors with better and more attractive investment terms than for more formal investors that you hope to attract during the growth stage of your business.

Financing the seed stage continued

2 PRIVATE SAVINGS

A small percentage of entrepreneurs have put money aside while doing other work, to enable the injection of funds into their prized idea. This is an ideal scenario. Bezos was fortunate to have just left a job as a hedge fund analyst earning more than $1 million so presumably he had some access to savings.

3 CREDIT CARDS

One of the fastest developing trends in the last decade, fueled by the demands of the dot.com world where speed of growth is so essential, has been the use of the credit card to fund small businesses. There are a lot of anecdotes from successful companies about how they survived the conception stages by "maxing out their credit cards."

ADVANTAGES OF CREDIT CARDS

1 Obtaining a credit card is much easier than getting a bank loan that requires extensive documentation and well-written forecasts of future business developments.

2 Getting credit on a card is also much quicker than waiting for approval of a loan request.

3 The cut-throat competition for credit card users has meant that companies have been offering highly attractive rates to potential clients, even though the era of o percent interest is on the wane (or at least, extra charges have been levied).

4 The social costs of borrowing from friends and family members are avoided with credit cards. You also avoid any intrusive queries into the state of the business.

Financing the seed stage continued

DISADVANTAGES OF CREDIT CARDS

1 The use of personal credit cards can be high, especially when periods of special offers end and interest rates are cranked up.

2 Gathering credit on different pieces of plastic can become addictive, especially as an entrepreneur isn't held accountable for the progress of the business.

3 Nonpayment of interest can begin to have negative effects on more traditional and structured ways of borrowing money.

TIPS TO SURVIVE THE USE OF CREDIT CARDS

1 Pay cards off every month to avoid charges. Even better, try to pay off the balance in full through a balance transfer with another card that, as yet, has no outstanding principal.

2 Replace the cards as soon as possible by more traditional bank financing and/or leasing arrangements, once the firm has reached the breakeven point and monthly sales receipts can cover normal overhead expenses and the cost of purchasing goods.

Financing the start-up stage

WHAT IS IT?

A business has reached the start-up stage when the seed of the initial business proposition has flowered and the company has officially launched, even though this may be modest.

In the case of Bezos, the first move was to incorporate the name "Amazon" in the state of Washington in 1994. Then it was to set up shop, in the garage of a two-bedroom house. Bezos reputedly created three micro stations on tables made out of doors. On July 16, 1995, Bezos opened his site to the world and in the first month, without any publicity, Amazon had sold books in all 50 U.S. states and in 45 foreign countries.

THE CHALLENGE

Entrepreneurs are by nature optimistic and at this start-up stage, even those who have the dramatic start-up success of an Amazon.com, may be facing their first dose of reality.

1 They may have underestimated the amount of cash flow needed to survive the first few months while invoices and sales receipts are paid.

2 They may have been too optimistic about the time it will take to sell their products or services either to an established market or to a market (as in Amazon.com) that doesn't yet exist.

Financing the start-up stage continued

THE CONDITIONS

In order for stage two of your financing resources to happen, you will ideally be in the following position:

1 The business has been formally launched and has a registered trading name.

2 You have manufactured some units of your product (if applicable), and you have achieved some sales of your product or services over several weeks, if not months.

3 You have established some sort of customer base, and have at least a minimal percentage of returning customers.

4 You are in a position to track down what aspects of the business are proving more profitable than others, as well as those that are proving more costly to operate.

5 You can write a detailed business report to show prospective financiers how your company has performed so far and what the prospects are for the next six months or, even better, a year.

Financing the start-up stage continued

SOURCES OF FINANCE

BANKING

The first places small business owners think of when looking for institutional financing are banks. These include

1 LARGE COMMERCIAL BANKS

ADVANTAGES

- Traditionally unfriendly to start-ups, attitudes are changing within larger banks. As loans to small business become increasingly competitive, larger banks are creating small business departments.

- They are at the forefront of developing technology, allowing them to reduce the time and cost of their loan application processing.

DISADVANTAGES

- Historically, banks have favored "big" small businesses with a proven track record. They aren't prone to taking risks.

- Large banks remain conservative lenders and require significant documentation and often 100 percent collateral to back a loan.

2   SMALL, COMMUNITY BANKS

ADVANTAGES
- Small, community banks offer your best option for conventional small business finance. They tend to be less formulaic in assessing loan applications and tend to be more willing to consider individual factors.

- It's easier to establish an ongoing working relationship with a community bank. The more familiar the lender is with the borrower, the greater the chances that the lender will understand and accommodate the individual needs of the small business.

DISADVANTAGES
- If the company's ambitions go beyond your immediate community, smaller banks may be reluctant to get involved.

Financing the start-up stage continued

TIPS FOR TAKING OUT BANK LOANS

1

WHAT IS THE LENGTH OF YOUR LOAN?

Interest rates tend to be higher than on short-term borrowing. They also require more substantial collateral as security against the extended duration of the lender's risk. Therefore, you have to decide whether you need a long-term or short-term loan.

SHORT-TERM debt is usually used to raise cash for working capital or cyclical inventory needs. If you know these debts can be paid off as soon as you get those sales receipts paid, then this is the option you should take as it is generally cheaper.

LONG-TERM debt is more often used to buy or improve existing assets such as equipment. As you know the business is going to benefit long-term from these improvements or acquisitions, you can afford to match the length of the loan (which is more expensive than a short-term loan) with the useful life of the asset.

2

IS YOUR DEBT SECURED OR UNSECURED?

A SECURED loan is when you offer up adequate collateral (a home, an office, or equipment that you own) as a guarantee for the loan. That way, the lender is "secure" that he will be able to seize a specific asset if you can't pay back the debt.

An UNSECURED loan is a promise to pay back the debt without granting the creditor an interest in a specific property.

Whichever path you take will depend on your creditworthiness. If you don't have a track record of paying back debt, you may be forced to take a secured loan. If you do have an established credit history, you may prefer not to put any of your assets at risk and take out an unsecured loan.

Financing the start-up stage continued

3 WHAT ARE YOUR OTHER COSTS?

The final cost of borrowing money often involves much more than just the interest rate. There could be other costs to consider that sway you against a particular loan. Try and answer the following:

- What are the penalty charges for not meeting loan repayments or for delayed payments?
- Will you be forced to present periodic financial reporting?
- Do you need personal guarantees to obtain the loan?

If the answer is "yes" to any of these questions, you may decide you don't have the time or that the direct or indirect costs are too high.

LEASING

Leasing allows you to obtain assets such as equipment or office space for a specified period in return for a monthly payment.

ADVANTAGES

1 Leasing reduces your upfront cash outlay, freeing up funds to finance other expenditures.

2 Leasing costs are deductible expenses, thereby reducing the amount of your taxable income.

DISADVANTAGES

1 The ultimate cost of the equipment for the period of the lease can be far higher than buying at the outset.

2 Even though you can write off payments, you are not allowed to deduct the depreciation.

Financing the start-up stage continued

FACTORING

Factoring is when a third party (factor) gives you cash (often within 24 hours) for accounts receivable. You pay a percentage of the invoice (known as an advance rate).

ADVANTAGES

1 You get discounts with your vendors for paying bills sooner.

2 Once the relationship matures, you can push for better terms.

DISADVANTAGES

1 You get only a percentage of the face value of each invoice—usually 75 to 90 percent. The rest arrives when your client pays up.

2 For an invoice due in 30 days, a factor may charge 2–6 percent.

TRADE CREDIT

Vendors or suppliers offer a form of financing called trade credit when they allow the buyer of their product or service to delay payment or to pay the bill in installments.

ADVANTAGES

1 It enables the buyer to spread payments over months or years.

2 There is minimal, or no, down payment and no interest charges.

DISADVANTAGES

1 The supplier may demand a priority security interest in all goods provided on credit.

2 You may have to guarantee some of the purchase price.

Financing the growth stage

WHAT IS IT?

Your company has reached the growth stage when you have seen customers and revenues increase consistently over a few months. In the case of Amazon.com, the growth stage was only two months, with book sales of $20,000 a week. Perhaps posting your first profits is another indication of growth, although this stage may take longer. Amazon.com is an example of a company that grew dramatically without actually posting profits.

THE CHALLENGE

Growth companies may have achieved several milestones, like establishing regular revenues and a client base, but in turn, these markers may also present a new range of operational and financial challenges.

1 You may have been so busy reaching initial target that now that the company is growing steadily, you don't have enough personnel to keep up with the increasing number of orders. Failing to satisfy an existing customer base can thwart future growth.

2 With added personnel, the burden is higher on extra office machinery. You may also need more equipment to provide for the next stage of products and services that clients demand.

In the case of Amazon.com, technological progress was paramount. Bezos and his team had to continue improving the site, introducing such unheard-of features at the time as one-click shopping, customer reviews, and e-mail order verification. The need for a continuous injection of capital was vital.

Financing the growth stage continued

THE CONDITIONS

As you approach your third round of financial backers, you will ideally be able to demonstrate to potential sources of finance that you meet the following conditions:

1 The company has at least a 12-month record of sales, preferably showing a progressive rise in revenue.

2 The company has a detailed project management plan that shows how the company intends to continue growing and what profits potential investors can expect to gain in return for their injection of more capital. Ideally investors can expect profits to be broken down into short- and long-term amounts and note the scale of the investment package.

3 Two related factors may help at this stage:

PREVIOUS FUNDING: If you can prove that you have already received a significant injection of capital (from one of the start-up financial sources, for example) into the project, you may get further backing.

FUTURE POTENTIAL: From the return on investment earned by the start-up investor(s), you can demonstrate a likely return on investment for a potential source of growth finance: this can encourage wavering investors to back you.

Financing the growth stage continued

ANGEL INVESTOR

WHAT IS IT?

An angel investor ("business angel" in Europe) is a wealthy individual—often a retired business owner or executive who hands over capital to a new business in return for the ownership of equity.

Unlike venture capitalists, angel investors don't tend to manage the pooled money of others in a professionally managed fund. However, angel investors often organize themselves into angel networks or angel groups to share research and to pool their own funds to make larger investments.

CASE STUDY

Early on in Amazon.com's history, Jeff Bezos was desperate to raise $1 million to finance the development of the web site and recruit the necessary experts. Although the sum was far higher than the average start-up usually needs, it was too low to attract interest from venture capital funds, given that Bezos had no track record of starting up companies.

With the backing of $100,000 from his parents, Bezos used his contacts in Silicon Valley to meet up with more than 60 angel investors. He was asking for a minimum of $50,000 from each. He ended up raising money from about 22 different angel investors, a considerable feat in the mid 1990s before the dot.com boom.

BENEFITS

■ VALUE ADDED CAPITAL
In addition to providing badly needed funds, angel investors, who are often highly experienced businessmen, can provide valuable management advice and important contacts.

■ ACCESS
At a critical growth period, angel investors can provide capital once a start-up has exhausted the friends and family option or faced limits from traditional lenders. Most venture capital funds will not consider investments under $1–2 million.

ALERTS

■ HIGH COSTS
As the risks at this stage of the business are very high, the angel investor will be seeking equally high returns, on the order of between 10 and 20 times the original investment over a period of five years.

■ CAREFUL PLANNING NEEDED
Angel investors will expect you to have defined a growth plan that may include an acquisition or an initial public offering (see pp. 150–153) that will bring high returns. These demands are, in effect, beneficial to your business.

Financing the growth stage continued

VENTURE CAPITAL FUNDS

WHAT IS IT?

Venture capital partners (also known as venture capitalists or VCs) are commonly large institutions seeking to invest considerable amounts of capital into growing businesses through a series of investment vehicles that include state and private pension funds, university endowments, and insurance companies.

Among the thousands of potential investments VCs look at a year, the most likely candidates are three- to five-year-old companies with the potential to offer higher-than-average profits to their shareholders. They need to have a competitive advantage in their sector and prove to have quality management.

Amazon.com passed both tests, as well as being innovative, and shortly after receiving angel investment of $1 million, managed to garner $8 million from blue chip venture capital firm Kleiner Perkins Caufield & Byers. Other well-known VC firms include: Draper Fisher Jurveston, Mayfield Fund, New Enterprise Associates, Sequoia Capital, Menlo Ventures Accel, and Garage Technology Ventures. VCs can be contacted directly, although it is more common to be approached through referrals.

BENEFITS

■ VOTE OF CONFIDENCE
If you succeed in receiving backing from VCs, it shows that your business is recognized as having growth potential. VCs turn down the majority of potential candidates, even when referred.

■ OUTSIDE EXPERTISE
Make use of experienced support from one of the VC general partners, who may join your Board of Directors. Also known as a mentor capitalist, he can help with general strategy.

ALERTS

■ SHARE DECISIONS
Be prepared to relinquish some decision-making power. Although VCs prefer passive influence, they can react when a business does not perform and insist on changes.

■ BE REALISTIC
Don't overestimate your chances of being suitable for VCs. They are very selective. Your chances are highest in fast-growing technology sectors.

■ READY FOR CHALLENGE?
Be ready to fulfill your business potential. VCs expect to sell their stock in your company within three to seven years, so you will be under much pressure to perform.

Financing the growth stage continued

INITIAL PUBLIC OFFERING

WHAT IS IT?

An initial public offering (IPO) is the sale of equity in a company, generally in the form of shares of common stock, through an investment banking firm. For smaller companies, shares will most typically trade on the Nasdaq SmallCap market or the Nasdaq National Market System.

Amazon.com's path to an IPO is not typical of most emerging companies as it occurred less than two years after it began its service. It was also part of the dramatic rise of IPOs among dot.com companies toward the end of the 1990s, most of which got badly burned.

IDEAL CANDIDATES

1 Your company needs to raise more than $5 million and you've exhausted your angel investors and VCs: the latter will likely have anticipated a potential IPO in your development.

2 You have to demonstrate minimum earnings growth potential of around 20 percent per year and the company will be expected to achieve a valuation of at least $100 million.

3 You must be able to show audited financials for the past several years.

4 You must operate in a high-profile industry (although qualifying as a dot.com today doesn't receive the instant acclaim of the late 1990s "Internet rush").

Financing the growth stage continued

BENEFITS

- A public company has direct access to the capital markets (see pp. 154–157).

- Public companies can use their common stock to attract and retain good employees.

- Owners and founders are provided with an exit for selling their ownership holdings in the business.

- Public companies tend to be valued more highly than private companies.

ALERTS

■ IPOs are very expensive. Not only do you have to lay out a lot of money upfront to pay for lawyers, accountants, printing, and miscellaneous fees, but an IPO can also cost at least 25 percent of the company's equity. Fees and expenses can also climb to as much as 25 percent of the deal.

■ You have to prepare a prospectus report that summarizes every aspect of the company's operating life from the day it opened up for business until the date of the IPO.

■ You have to select an investment bank to handle the underwriting of the IPO. Sometimes, the IPO is handled by one investment bank. In exchange for accepting the full risk of selling the business's shares, the bank will charge a fee that is then deducted from the total funds raised.

Financing the mature stage

WHAT IS IT?

A company reaches the mature, or established, stage when its business has an established place in the market and can rely on loyal customers. In Amazon.com's case, a definite marker was when the company, after having faced years of skepticism about its business model, recorded its first annual profit in 2003.

CHALLENGE

Just because you've reached the point where your core business is consolidated does not mean you can rest on your laurels, especially in a marketplace that is constantly evolving, like the dot.com world. New challenges, as well as new opportunities for expansion, emerge all the time. In the case of Amazon.com, the company has diversified away from its core bookstore business to include retail sales of music CDs, videotapes and DVDs, software, consumer electronics, toys and games, baby products, and sporting goods, among other products. The maturity of its book and music business, however, helps to finance new product categories.

SOURCES OF FINANCE: CAPITAL MARKET SECURITIES

There are three basic types of securities that companies issue to raise capital:

1 COMMON STOCK

Investment banks help companies issue stock, which is a fractional ownership interest in the corporation. Owners of common stock are entitled to

- DIVIDENDS: The name for after-tax corporate earnings distributed to shareholders, these are normally paid in cash and on a quarterly basis.

- VOTING RIGHTS: Holders can vote on the selection of board members.

- RESIDUAL OWNERSHIP: When it comes to sharing profits, holders of common stock will be the last to get paid after creditors and bondholders.

2 PREFERRED STOCK

BENEFIT: The greatest advantage of holding preferred stock is that holders receive payment before common stock holders but after bondholders.

ALERT: Unlike bonds (see pp. 156–157), the U.S. tax code does not allow the corporation to deduct the dividend paid to shareholders so both common and preferred stock are not as popular with companies as bonds.

Financing the mature stage continued

3 BONDS

A bond is a loan that takes the form of a debt security. The borrower (known as the issuer) owes the holder (the lender) a debt and is obliged to repay the principal and interest (the coupon). The issuer may have to provide certain information on the company to the bond holder.

BENEFITS

- Bonds are viewed as safer investments than stocks because they suffer from less day-to-day volatility than stocks.

- Bonds' interest payments are higher than dividend payments that the same company is likely to pay to its stock holders.

- If you hold a bond, you have the certainty of a fixed interest payment twice a year.

- If a company goes into bankruptcy, its bond holders will often receive some money back, whereas the company's stock often ends up valueless.

ALERTS

- Although it isn't difficult to sell bond investments, it is easier to sell stocks.

- The market price of fixed rate bonds will tend to fall in value when the generally prevailing interest rate rises. This presents investors with other opportunities to get a good interest rate.

- The prices of bonds can become volatile if one of the credit rating agencies like Standard & Poor's or Moody's upgrades or downgrades the credit rating of the issuer.

- If the company goes bankrupt, bond holders are paid before stock holders but after bank lenders and deposit holders.

4 COMMERCIAL PAPER

This is a money market security issued by large banks and corporations for short-term investments (maximum nine months) such as purchases of inventory. These unsecured IOUs are considered safe, but returns are small.

Key terms

ANGEL INVESTOR: a wealthy individual, often a retired business owner or executive, who hands over capital to a new business in return for ownership equity.

BOND: a loan that takes the form of a debt security. The borrower (issuer) owes the holder (the lender) a debt and is obliged to repay the principal and interest (the coupon).

COMMERCIAL PAPER: a money market security issued by large banks and corporations for short-term investments (maximum nine months) such as purchases of inventory.

COMMON STOCK: a fractional ownership interest in a company.

COST-BENEFIT ANALYSIS: describes balancing the expected costs of launching or running a business against the expected benefits.

DEBT FINANCING: the borrowing of money, usually involving the accumulation of interest at some future date.

DIVIDENDS: after-tax corporate earnings distributed to shareholders, usually paid in cash and on a quarterly basis.

EQUITY FINANCING: an exchange of money or capital for a share of business ownership. This involves selling the future benefits and profits of your business to investors.

FACTORING: describes a loan by a third party (factor) given in the form of cash (often within 24 hours) for accounts receivable. The borrower pays a percentage of the invoice.

IPO: initial public offering; the sale of equity in a company, generally in the form of shares of common stock, through an investment banking firm.

PREFERRED STOCKS: holders of preferred stock receive payment before common stock holders but after bond holders.

SECURED LOAN: a loan that offers up adequate collateral (a home, an office, or equipment that you own) as a guarantee for the loan.

TRADE CREDIT: a form of financing when the vendor or supplier allows the buyer of their product or service to delay payment or to pay the invoice in installments.

VENTURE CAPITALISTS (VCs): commonly large institutions seeking to invest considerable amounts of capital into growing businesses through a series of investment vehicles that include state and private pension funds, university endowments, and insurance companies.

KEY TERMS

Key questions: Sources of finance

1

WHAT CHOICES DO YOU HAVE TO RAISE FUNDS?
1. DEBT FINANCING involves a loan that will accumulate future interest.
2. EQUITY FINANCING involves accepting a lump sum in exchange for selling the future benefits and profits of your business to investors.

2

WHAT MIX OF DEBT/EQUITY IS USED IN A BUSINESS LIFE CYCLE?
1. SEED STAGE
WHAT IS IT?: When your business is just a thought or an idea.
FINANCIAL SOURCES:
- Family and friends
- Private savings
- Credit cards: usually much quicker than waiting for a loan approval

2. START-UP STAGE
WHAT IS IT?: When the company has officially launched.
FINANCIAL SOURCES:
- Banking, typically the first option of small business owners
- Small, community banks
- Leasing: paying a monthly payment for renting assets like equipment or office space
- Factoring: paying an advance rate to a third party (factor) in exchange for cash
- Trade credit: when a supplier allows the buyer to delay payment

3. GROWTH STAGE

WHAT IS IT? When a business has successfully traded for a period.

FINANCIAL SOURCES:

- Angel investor: a wealthy individual who hands over capital in return for ownership equity.
- Venture capital funds: large institutions seeking to invest considerable amounts of capital into growing businesses through a series of investment vehicles.
- Initial public offering (IPO): the sale of equity in a company, generally in the form of shares of common stock, through an investment banking firm.

4. MATURE STAGE

WHAT IS IT? When its business has an established place in the market.

FINANCIAL SOURCES:

- Capital market securities such as common stock, dividends, voting rights.
- Bonds—loans that take the form of a debt security where the borrower (known as the issuer) owes the holder (the lender) a debt and is obliged to repay the principal and interest (the coupon).
- Commercial paper—a money market security issued by large banks and corporations for short-term investments (maximum nine months) such as purchases of inventory.

KEY QUESTIONS

5

interpreting financial
information

Benefits of interpreting financial data

1 KNOW YOUR MARKET

Many new businesses launch a product or service to the market without fully understanding whether there is sufficient demand, the total costs of the launch, and what prices they can reasonably charge. This is because they have ignored the importance of obtaining financial data and interpreting it.

2 MEASURE GROWTH

For a company to evaluate its growth plan, it needs to establish a way to tell when it has reached important points or milestones in the process. Without these benchmarks, it is difficult to analyze the health of the business and its future prospects.

3 MAKE AUTHORITATIVE DECISIONS

For many managers, decision making is made complicated by a lack of adequate information about their companies. They often lack enough data to be able to answer the following questions (if you have difficulty in answering at least half of the following questions, you too need to pay more attention to financial information):

- What is my most profitable product or service?
- What are the traits of my best customers?
- Which types of promotions have the highest payback?
- Do I know what will happen if sales volume drops? How far can it drop before we go into the red?
- If I lower our prices in order to sell more, how much more will I have to sell?
- If I take out a loan and our fixed costs rise because of the interest on the loan, what sales volume will I need in order to cover those increased costs?

Common benchmarks

1 SALES REVENUE
Many companies recognize the first year they topped $1 million, $5 million, and $10 million in sales because it is an easily grasped benchmark. For Amazon.com, the focus in the first five years was to sustain growth in sales and to diversify its products, rather than to achieve profits.

2 PROFITS
All companies aim to break even and then to garner profits. The key is that the profits continue to grow.

3 STORES
In an expansion phase, the physical growth of a company may be more important than sales because the company is investing in establishing a presence to achieve future growth.

4 CUSTOMERS
Establishing customer loyalty and repeat sales was also a measure of growth for a company like Amazon.com, even before achieving profits. Once these are established, the company can then assess further benchmarks such as:

■ Percentage of repeat customers: this can be expressed as a percentage of total customers, and in the case of a company like Amazon.com could be expected to continue to rise

■ Average sales per customer

■ Crossover from core product category (books) into other product categories the company was adding

interpreting financial information

Evaluating performance

The following section outlines the most typical methods companies can use to assess performance of investments and personnel, and their overall potential for growth.

COST-BENEFIT ANALYSIS

WHAT IS IT?
Cost-benefit analysis is basically weighing the expected costs of launching or running a business against the expected benefits. The costs involved are:

VARIABLE costs that are directly involved with the new activity. These differ from:

FIXED costs, which remain more or less the same, regardless of the new business.

These cover existing mortgage or rental repayments on the premises, a business license, any interest repayments on loans, and salaries of full-time workers.

HOW TO MEASURE

As an example, take a bookstore in a small, university town that is struggling to compete in two of its markets:

1 Student textbooks, which are cheaper in bigger academic book stores

2 General "light" fiction, which supermarkets are selling at heavily discounted prices

The company is considering a response that will involve clearing three aisles of space in order to

1 Create a coffeeshop/café within the store to offer customers more of a "leisure experience"

2 Introduce a new line of products: records and DVDs

Evaluating performance continued

WORK OUT COSTS

Write down the costs of the two projects (figures are made for illustrative purposes only).

FOR BOTH PROJECTS:
■ Cost of taking down shelves and refurbishing the area = $100,000

COFFEESHOP:
■ Cost of coffee-making machinery and furniture = $70,000
■ Cost of extra staff to service the café = $60,000

DVD:
■ Cost of buying new products = $100,000

BENEFITS

COFFEESHOP:
■ Direct revenue of coffeeshop (sales of beverages and pastries/snacks = $90,000)
■ Indirect revenue from new customers driven to store through coffeeshop

DVD:
■ Direct revenue from sales of DVDs = $110,000

At this stage, you should have a list of both the direct costs and benefits on the respective left- and right-hand columns of a blank piece of paper.

PAYBACK PERIOD

Payback period describes the time it will take for the capital outlay for the project to pay for itself. Typically, companies favor a payback period that lasts no more than two or three years: any longer makes less financial sense and makes securing finance more difficult.

COST OF PROJECT A
(COFFEESHOP) IS

$100,000 (for refurbishment) +
$70,000 (new machinery) +
$60,000 (staff) = $230,000

Projected annual cash flow =
$90,000

Calculation: $230,000 ÷ $90,000
= 2 years and 6 months

COST OF PROJECT B
(DVD PRODUCT LINE) IS

$100,000 (for refurbishment) +
$100,000 (cost of buying stock)
= $200,000

Projected annual cash flow =
$110,000

Calculation: $200,000 ÷ $110,000
= 1 year and 10 months

Evaluating performance continued

CONCLUSION:

Under the payback method of analysis, projects or purchases with shorter payback periods rank higher than those with longer paybacks because they are more liquid and less risky.

ALERT

This method does not take into account the following:

1. The initial investment into project A, the coffeshop, is far higher in the first year since it involves the purchase of extra equipment, but overheads go down in the second year, since the equipment is in place.

   By contrast, the overheads for project B, buying DVD stock, remain more or less constant: the store relies on replenishing stock as it is sold. There is also going to be a time lag between paying for DVD stock, and seeing a return on the investment, when the stock is sold.

2   The impact of the installation of the coffeshop on overall sales
    of the bookstore may prove beneficial in attracting
    nontraditional bookstore customers into the store and into
    developing a brand loyalty for the store.

    The introduction of DVDs may have less impact on book sales
    because the buyers of one product may not be customers for
    the other. These factors are less easy to quantify and yet may
    prove more of an incentive than actual figures.

Return on investment

Return on Investment (ROI) is another method of measuring the benefits of the project over time (when this is time specific) or in the case of the bookstore, over a year.

The formula is

Divide the net profit expected for the first year by the amount of expenditure and express it as a percentage of the outlay.

EXAMPLE

PROJECT A

Project A (coffeeshop) has a net profit of $90,000 and total capital of $230,000.

$90,000 \div 230,000 = 0.36 \times 100 = 36$ percent

PROJECT B

Project B (DVDs) has a net profit of $110,000 and total capital of $200,000.

$110,000 \div 200,000 = 0.55 \times 100 = 55$ percent

CONCLUSION

Under the ROI method of analysis, the higher percentage should be the most attractive rate. In this case, project B appears as the safest bet.

ALERT

1 As in the case of payback period analysis, this method does not take into account that the ROI may change in year two or year three, as outlays for the coffeeshop fall while expenditure on DVD products continues the same.

2 The percentage figure does not take into account the less easily quantifiable features of the coffeeshop such as its role as a magnet for achieving more browsing opportunities by customers in the bookstore's core products and, potentially, more sales.

interpreting financial information
Breakeven analysis

Payback period and ROI are most useful as early indicators of whether a project is viable or not. Once these simple methods have been tested, a related approach can be tried.

WHAT IS IT?

Breakeven analysis provides a way of finding out how many actual sales of either beverages and pastries (for project A) or sales of DVDs (for project B) are necessary to recoup the capital spent on the original investment. The following components are necessary in order to make the calculation:

CONTRIBUTION MARGINS

A company's contribution margin is the percentage of each sales dollar left over after the variable costs (those directly related to selling the product) are taken away from overall profits.
The formula is:
Contribution margin per unit = Sales price per unit (a cup of coffee or DVD) – Variable cost per unit

Assume each coffee sells for $2 and costs $0.50 to produce (variable cost). This means each cup of coffee contributes $1.50 to overall sales.

Assume each DVD retails at $8 and costs $6 to purchase (variable cost). This means each DVD contributes $2 to overall sales.

BREAKEVEN VOLUME
Formula: Breakeven volume = Variable costs/Contribution margin per unit

PROJECT A

Breakeven volume =
$230,000/$1.50 = 153,000

The bookstore will have to sell
more than 153,000 cups of coffee
units in its first year (or 1,275 a
month) to recoup its initial
investment of $230,000.

PROJECT B

Breakeven volume =
$200,000/$2 = 100,000

The bookstore will have to sell
100,000 DVDs in its first year (or
833 a month) to recoup its
$200,000 investment.

interpreting financial information

The time value of money

The problem with the methods mentioned—cost-benefit, payback, return on investment, and breakeven analysis—is that they don't take into account the "time value" of money.

TIME VALUE describes the concept that a dollar received today is worth more than a dollar received at some point in the future, because the dollar received today can be invested and starts to attract interest. This is a harsh reminder for decision makers that the future benefits, when they arrive, may be worth less dollar for dollar than if the initial capital outlay was put in, for example, an investment fund.

NET PRESENT VALUE method (NPV) helps you to estimate the present value in today's currency of the future net cash flow of your project.

HOW TO CALCULATE
First you need to specify an interest rate that you can use as the discount rate that you apply to the future benefits forecasted. The rate could be between 5 and 18 percent, but for the purposes of clarity, we will assume a rate of 10 percent.

NOTE TO CALCULATE
A decision maker will typically insist that a project's earnings should exceed the cost of borrowing, to compensate for the project's related risk, time, and trouble.

PROJECT A

Using payback calculations, the project will be profitable after 2.5 years.

Estimate the interest accumulated if the capital outlay of $230,000 had simply accumulated at 10 percent interest rate a year:
$23,000 a year x 2.5 years = $57,500

The projected revenue of project A = $90,000. To this sum, you have to assume a discount rate of 10 percent a year for the 2.5 years = 10,000 x 2.5= $25,000.

Today's value of projected revenue = 90,000 – 25,000 = $65,000

The result is that the business has made $1,000 less than if the original capital had been invested in a high-interest savings account.

PROJECT B

Using payback analysis, the project should reap profits after 22 months (say 2 years for the purposes of this illustration).

Estimate the interest accumulated if the capital outlay of $200,000 had simply accumulated at 10 percent interest rate a year:
$20,000 a year x 2 years = $40,000

The projected revenue of project B = $110,000. To this sum, you have to assume a discount rate of 10 percent a year:
10,000 x 2 = $20,000.

Today's value of projected revenue = 110,000 – 20,000 = $90,000. The result is that the business has made $70,000 more than if the original capital had been invested in a high-interest savings account.

Valuing the company

Valuing a business is never an exact science with no one right way of determining a company's price. There are three common ways of appraising a business.

1. HARD NUMBERS
These are based on existing financial figures and include

1

EQUITY BOOK VALUE
The simple formula is to subtract a company's liabilities from its assets based on historical records.

2

ADJUSTED BOOK VALUE
This is the same formula but takes into account the fair market value of assets and liabilities, which may produce a more accurate picture as historical records may be very out-of-date.

LIQUIDATION VALUE
This is another variation on the balance sheet theme that calculates how much money is left when assets are sold quickly and debts are paid off.

FAIR MARKET VALUE
This is simply the value established between a willing buyer and a willing seller.

MARKET VALUE
This applies to a publicly traded company.

Valuing the company continued

2. SOFT NUMBERS

Soft numbers are based on estimates of future benefits and therefore contain an element of subjectivity.

1 INCOME METHOD
This is a measurement of the future benefits such as sales, profits, or cost savings.

2 DISCOUNTED CASH FLOW APPROACH
This approach brings future anticipated income to present value.

3 INVESTMENT VALUE
This takes into account the special benefits that a buyer accrues from acquiring the new entity.

INTANGIBLE ASSETS

Increasingly, prospective buyers are putting a greater onus on a company's intangible assets, which include people, knowledge, relationships, intellectual property, brand names, loyal customer base, copyrights or trademarks, proprietary mailing lists, long-term contracts, and franchises.

Some intangible assets can be priced using traditional approaches such as

1 COST-BASED VALUATION
How much would it cost you to duplicate some of these assets today?

2 MARKET-BASED VALUATION
What were the sale transactions of brand-named goods in the sector?

3 CUSTOMER-DRIVEN VALUATION
What is the value of a loyal customer? What does the average customer spend per purchase a year? How long has he been a customer?

MARKET COMPETITION

Research into the company and its place in its sector are also relevant. Is your business in a growth industry or a declining one?

Key terms

ADJUSTED BOOK VALUE: takes into account the fair market value of assets and liabilities that may produce a more accurate picture as historical records may be very out-of-date.

BREAKEVEN ANALYSIS: a way of finding out how many actual sales of a particular product are necessary to recoup the capital spent on the original investment.

BREAKEVEN VOLUME: variable costs divided by contribution margin per unit.

CONTRIBUTION MARGIN: the percentage of each sales dollar left over after the variable costs are taken away from overall profits.

EQUITY BOOK VALUE: the difference between a company's liabilities and its assets, based on historical records.

FAIR MARKET VALUE: the value established between a willing buyer and a willing seller.

FIXED COSTS: costs that remain more or less the same, regardless of the new business.

LIQUIDATION VALUE: another variation on the balance sheet theme that calculates how much money is left when assets are sold quickly and debts are paid off.

NPV: net present value, which describes the present value in today's currency of the future net cash flow of your project.

PAYBACK PERIOD: the time it will take for the capital outlay for the project to pay for itself.

RETURN ON INVESTMENT (ROI): a method used to measure the benefits of the project over the length of time of a project (when this is time specific) or in the case of the bookstore, over a year.

SOFT NUMBERS: estimates of future benefits; they contain an element of subjectivity.

TIME VALUE: the concept that a dollar received today is worth more than a dollar received at some point in the future because the dollar received today can be invested to earn interest.

VARIABLE COSTS: costs that are directly involved with the new activity.

KEY TERMS

Summary: Financial information

1 WHY INTERPRET FINANCIAL DATA?

It helps to know your markets, measure growth, and make authoritative decisions.

2 WHAT ARE COMMON BENCHMARKS?

Sales revenues, profits, number of stores, and customers.

3 HOW DO YOU EVALUATE PERFORMANCE?

COST-BENEFIT ANALYSIS

WHAT IS IT? You weigh the expected costs of launching or running a business against the expected benefits. The costs involved are variable (directly involved with the new activity) and fixed (these remain more or less the same, regardless of the new business).

RETURN ON INVESTMENT

WHAT IS IT? A method used to measure the benefits of the project over the length of time of a project (when this is time specific) or in the case of the bookstore, over a year.

You divide the net profit expected for the first year by the amount of expenditure and express it as a percentage of the outlay.

BREAKEVEN ANALYSIS
WHAT IS IT? It provides a way of finding out how many sales are
necessary to recoup the capital spent on the original investment. You
need to know your contribution margin (the percentage of each sales
dollar left over after variable costs are taken away from overall profits).

TIME VALUE OF MONEY
WHAT IS IT? It describes the concept that a dollar received today is
worth more than a dollar received at some point in the future
because the dollar received today can be invested to earn interest.
The harsh reality is that future benefits may be worth less dollar for
dollar than if the capital outlay was put in an investment fund.

WHAT ARE THE WAYS TO VALUE A COMPANY?
HARD NUMBERS. These are based on existing figures and include
equity book value (assets minus liabilities) and fair market value (the
value established between a willing buyer and a willing seller).

SOFT NUMBERS. These are based on estimates of future benefits and
therefore contain an element of subjectivity.

INTANGIBLE ASSETS. These include people, knowledge, relationships,
intellectual property, brand names, loyal customer base, copyrights or
trademarks, mailing lists, long-term contracts, and franchises.

KEY QUESTIONS

6

taxes and taxation

Business structures and tax

What kind of business structure best suits your business for tax purposes? This is a key question facing most companies, particularly start-ups. A tax professional is best placed to give advice on the intricacies of the complex and, in many ways, arcane U.S. tax code. However, this section aims to outline some general issues about business taxation and how to keep on the right side of the IRS, the U.S. government agency responsible for tax collection, and the enforcement of tax law.

The following are the main business structures for a company and their specific tax advantages and disadvantages.

SOLE PROPRIETORSHIP

WHAT IS IT?

This is the easiest and quickest way of setting up a business operation as there are no blanket prerequisites nor any specific costs in starting a sole proprietorship. You are the sole owner. Unless your spouse, for instance, is vested with one-half interest, you have full control and responsibility for the business operation. When filing their annual tax returns with the IRS, sole proprietors (or self-employed people) are required to list their business income and business expenses on a Schedule C, or possibly a Schedule C-EZ, of their individual tax returns.

TAX ADVANTAGES

It is easier, faster, and less expensive than filing any other type of business tax return. The limit on business expenses now stands at $5,000.

You can generally prepare returns yourself, without the added time and expense of hiring a tax professional to do it for you.

DISADVANTAGES

You cannot carry any inventory, you have to make a profit, you can't hire an employee, and you can't claim expenses for the business use of your home.

You have a much higher chance of being audited by the IRS, particularly when the Schedule C contains a deduction for a home office or the income and expenses are significant dollar amounts.

Legally, you have unlimited personal liability for anything that goes wrong in your business. Your personal and business assets are at risk.

Business structures and tax continued

PARTNERSHIP

WHAT IS IT?

A partnership is a business form created when two or more persons get together in a business enterprise for profit. As in the case of sole proprietorship, there are no costs or formalities required. They are the only business entities that can be formed by oral agreement or a mere handshake, although it is advisable to prepare a document with the help of an attorney. There are various forms of partnership including:

GENERAL PARTNERSHIP

In a general partnership, all partners share in the management of the entity and share in the entity's profits. Partners are also personally liable for its debts.

LIMITED PARTNERSHIP

This is a more complex structure as it is owned by two classes of partners. General partners, as in a general partnership, are managers of the enterprise and liable for debts. Limited partners provide capital and get a share in the profits but don't get involved with the management of the company. Limited partners are not liable for partnership debts. With the rise of the limited liability company (see below), limited partnerships are on the wane.

LIMITED LIABILITY PARTNERSHIP

The limited liability partnership (LLP) comprises licensed professionals such as attorneys, accountants. and architects. Partners are not liable for the acts of other partners but are liable for their own actions.

DVANTAGES

Partnerships enjoy the same tax advantages as sole proprietorships. It is important to note that the partnership itself is not taxed. The partners pay tax on their own proportion of the profits of the company, regardless of whether those profits are distributed or reinvested. This is known as pass-through or flow-through taxation.

They don't have to pay minimum taxes required of corporations and limited liability companies (see pp. 184–187 and 201–203).

SADVANTAGES

All owners are subject to unlimited personal liability for the debts, losses, and liabilities of the business (except in cases of limited partnerships and limited liability partnerships).

Taxation is the same as for a corporation, but in a partnership individual partners bear responsibility for the actions of other partners.

Business structures and tax continued

CORPORATION

WHAT IS IT?

Unlike a partnership, a corporation (known as C corporation) is an artificially created legal entity that is considered to exist separately from the one or more individuals who created it.

Corporations are most commonly managed by appointed or elected officers. This is known as representative management.

To form a corporation, you simply file an application for a charter. This application should state

- the names and addresses of the incorporators
- the business purpose of the intended corporation
- the amount and types of stock the corporation will issue
- the rights and privileges that can be expected by the holder of each class of stock

ONTAX ADVANTAGES

1 UNLIMITED LIFE
Unlike proprietorships and partnerships, the life of the corporation is not dependent on the life of a particular individual or individuals.

2 EASILY TRANSFERRED SHARES
To divest yourself of ownership in proprietorships and partnerships can be expensive and difficult, whereas your ownership interest in a business can be easily sold, transferred, or given away to a family member. This is attractive to potential investors.

3 NO LIABILITY
Shareholders are not legally liable for the actions of the corporation.

Business structures and tax continued

NONTAX DISADVANTAGES

1 The business owners are responsible for additional recordkeeping requirements and administrative details with the corresponding burden on costs.

2 The unlimited "shelf life" of the corporation can lead to stagnation. If management lacks dynamism, there is no force for change, diversification, and increased market share.

X ADVANTAGE

Most large corporations are classified as C corporations and subject to corporate taxes. Corporations are taxed on income and, as long as it can be proved they are for business purposes, a corporation can subtract expenses from its revenues. The more common legitimate business expenses are listed on pp. 224–225.

X DISADVANTAGE

Double taxation is the biggest tax burden for corporations. Any profits passed on to shareholders are effectively taxed twice: once under the banner of "corporate income" and then again as part of personal income.

Business structures and tax continued

"S" CORPORATIONS

WHAT IS IT?

An S corporation is a hybrid form of corporation that is particularly attractive to small private companies because it shares some of the appealing tax benefits enjoyed by partnerships, while providing business owners with the liability protection that corporations benefit from.

TAX ADVANTAGES

1 The main reason a small company will opt for S corporation status is because it will be exempt from corporate tax liability avoiding the dreaded double taxation. Shareholders are only taxed on their individual tax returns.

2 Owners of S corporations who don't have inventory can use the cash method of accounting, which is simpler than the accrual method (see pp. 16–19). Under this method, income is taxable when received, and expenses are deductible when paid.

HOW TO BE ELIGIBLE FOR S STATUS

1 The corporation must have no more than 75 shareholders. A husband and wife count as one shareholder in calculating the total limit of 75 shareholders.

2 S corporations cannot have non-U.S. citizens as shareholders.

3 S corporations have to file articles of incorporation, hold directors and shareholders meetings, keep corporate minutes, and allow shareholders to vote on major corporate decisions.

Business structures and tax continued

4 S corporations can only issue common stock, making it more difficult to raise capital than a C corporation.

5 To gain an S status, a corporation has to make the Subchapter S election no later than two months and 15 days after the first day of the taxable year. All shareholders have to consent to Subchapter S election.

6 States differ in their treatment of S corporations with some, for instance, offering no tax break at all and others requiring the filing of a state-specific form.

7 An S corporation may revoke its Subchapter S status by either failing to meet the conditions of eligibility for S corporations or by filing with the IRS no later than two months and 15 days after the first day of the taxable year.

LIMITED LIABILITY COMPANIES

Although the S corporation is a logical route for many small businesses trying to avoid the potential tax pitfalls of C corporations, the limited liability company (LLC) is increasingly becoming a popular alternative.

An LLC is a hybrid entity that has the legal protection of a corporation and the advantage of being taxed, like a partnership, only once. You can form an LLC for any lawful business as long as the nature of the business is not banking, insurance, and certain other professional service operations.

TAX SIMILARITIES WITH S CORPORATIONS

Both LLCs and S corporations enjoy pass-through taxation, which allows the income or loss generated by the company to be reflected on owners or shareholders' personal income tax returns. They both avoid double taxation.

Business structures and tax continued

NONTAX ADVANTAGES OF LLCS OVER S CORPORATIONS

1 An LLC can have an unlimited number of members (owners), unlike an S corporation, which is restricted to no more than 75 shareholders.

2 Unlike a partnership, an LLC can be owned by C corporations, other S corporations, and many trusts and other LLCs.

3 Distributing profits at LLCs is easier. An LLC can have many different types of interest and the percentage of pass-through income is not tied to ownership percentage, unlike the case of S corporations.

4   LLCs are also more flexible in distributing profits than S corporations, wherein the corporation can only have one class of stock and your percentage of ownership determines the percentage of pass-through income. On the other hand, an LLC can have many different classes of interest, and the percentage of pass-through income is not tied to ownership percentage. The pass-through percentage can be set by agreement of the members in the LLC's operating agreement.

ONTAX DISADVANTAGES OF LLCS OVER S CORPORATIONS

1   Two people at least are required to form an LLC, while one person can form an S corporation.

2   The stock of S corporations is freely transferrable, while the interest (ownership) of LLCs is not.

Business tax issues

This section covers the multitude of tax issues that affect you as the owner of a business.

Regardless of whether they use a cash or accrual method of accounting (see Chapter 2), all taxpayers follow a system of annual accounting based on the calendar year. Income taxes are always levied on a year-by-year basis, and each year is "compartmentalized" from both the previous year and the following year.

INCOME TAX

PERSONAL

Personal income tax in the United States is progressive. As taxable income rises, a progressively higher rate is applied. The following are some examples for single taxpayers.

The first $7,550 of taxable income is charged 10 percent.

After the first $7,550, the rate applied is a flat $755 (10 percent of the first $7,550), plus 15 percent of the amount over $7,550.

The next progressive tier is reached at $30,650 where the percentage goes up again (to 25 percent).

Business tax issues continued

CORPORATE
Tax rates for corporate income is also progressive and works in several tiers.

Most corporations (see pp. 194–197) determine their tax using the following schedule.

1 Up to $50,000: 15 percent

2 $50,000 to $75,000: $7,500 plus 25 percent of the amount over $50,00c

3 $75,000 to $100,000: $13,750 plus 34 percent of the amount over $75,00

4 $100,000 to $335,000: $22,250 plus 39 percent of the amount over $100,00

5 $335,000 to $10 million: $113,900 plus 34 percent of the amount over $335,000

$10 million to $15 million: $3.4 million plus 35 percent of the amount over $10 million

$15 million to $18,333,333: $5.15 million plus 38 percent of the amount over $15 million

$18,333,333 and above: 35 percent

r corporation may be subject to several other taxes including:

Accumulated-earnings tax

Distribution of income to individual stockholders is taxable a second time as ordinary dividend income. This double taxation is effectively eliminated as long as the company files a Subchapter S election with the IRS (see pp.198–200).

Business tax issues continued

SOCIAL SECURITY AND MEDICARE TAXES

In addition to income tax, all self-employed individuals and employers have to pay Social Security and Medicare taxes.

1

SELF-EMPLOYED

Individuals who are self-employed (a category that typically includes the owners of an operating partnership or a limited liability company) are legally required to pay a 15.3 percent combined Social Security and Medicare tax up to a designated limit. This percentage is more than employees pay, because an employer matches an employee's contribution, effectively doubling it. The percentage is far less after about $70,000.

EMPLOYERS

If you have one or more employees, you are legally required to withhold income tax and Social Security tax from each employee's paycheck and remit these amounts to the appropriate agency.

As an employer you have to match each of your employees' contributions dollar for dollar. Typically, employees pay a 7.65 percent combined tax rate—that is, 6.2 percent in Social Security tax and 1.45 percent in Medicare—up to the designated limit.

Business tax issues continued

UNEMPLOYMENT/INCOME TAX

Employers also have to pay unemployment tax in most states. The tax is worked out as a percentage of your total payroll (up to a specified limit of annual wage per employee) and remitted at the end of each quarter. The actual percentage varies from state to state and by type of employer.

You are also responsible for deducting income tax from each employee's paycheck.

TIP: Always check if your worker is officially an employee or an independent contractor. You are not responsible for paying Social Security/Medicare or unemployment taxes for independent contractors.

Workers are independent contractors if you don't have a direct control over the way they carry out their duties. To avoid any future misunderstandings, it's best to get them to sign a contract stating that they are doing work for you as an independent contractor.

CAPITAL GAINS TAX

Both individuals and businesses are subject to capital gains tax, which occurs when an investment or business asset (other than inventory) is sold at a gain. Capital gain rates vary between 8 and 20 percent.

The asset most likely to incur a substantial capital gains tax liability occurs if the business itself is sold for a profit during the company owner's lifetime.

SALES TAXES

Sales taxes are collected at varying rates in different states so you will have to contact your state or local revenue offices for information on the law for your particular area.

Business tax issues continued

TAX CREDITS
Your income tax bill can be
minimized if you are eligible to
claim tax credits.

BENEFITS
Tax credits are favorable to tax
deductions (see pp. 214–227) for
the following reasons:

1 They are taken away from your tax bill while deductions are
subtracted from the income that makes up your tax bill.

2 A dollar's worth of tax credit reduces your tax bill by a dollar.
A dollar's worth of deductions can lower you tax bill by 38
cents if you are in the 38 percent bracket, by 32 cents if you
are in a 32 percent bracket, and so forth.

ERT

Tax credits are very difficult to obtain and apply only to certain sectors like energy and leisure and entertainment (particularly restaurants, bars, and hotels).

These are the most common personal tax credits:
- Adoption Tax Credit
- Child and Dependent Care Tax Credit
- Child Tax Credit
- Earned Income Tax Credit
- Foreign Tax Credit
- Credit for the Elderly and Disabled
- Hope Tax Credit
- Lifetime Learning Tax Credit
- Mortgage Interest Tax Credit

Tax credits

The following list includes credits that are most beneficial to businesses:

1 CREDIT FOR FICA TAX ON TIPS
If you run a business where employees are tipped by customers, then you are entitled to a tax credit for any Social Security and Medicare (FICA) taxes.

2 GASOLINE TAX CREDIT
If gasoline forms a major part of your transport costs, and these are integral to your business, then you can claim a credi for any federal excise taxes you pay on gasoline and special fuels (such as heating oil, liquified petroleum gas, and compressed natural gas).

3 FOREIGN TAX CREDIT
If you are liable for foreign taxes on profits from overseas operations or investments, you can claim a credit for foreign income taxes.

CREDITS BENEFITING DISADVANTAGED GROUPS

The government also encourages private business to provide jobs for disadvantaged groups by offering credits for the following:

WORK OPPORTUNITY TAX CREDIT

Companies receive a credit if they hire people who hail from groups with unusually high unemployment rates such as

- war veterans whose families receive food stamps

- families on cash welfare benefits for at least nine months

- urban youths (aged 18–24) considered high risk

- ex-convicts who are members of low-income families

Tax credits continued

2 WELFARE-TO-WORK TAX CREDIT
This is aimed at providing work for recipients of qualified long-term family assistance (such as Aid to Families with Dependent Children (AFDC) or its successor program).

3 DISABLED ACCESS CREDIT
To help companies comply with rules that force them to accommodate or help people with disabilities, credits are awarded to companies for removing physical barriers and also for providing services for deaf, blind, and other disabled workers.

4 EMPOWERMENT ZONE EMPLOYMENT CREDIT
Tax incentives are awarded to workers who live within certain designated parts of key U.S. cities.

INDIAN EMPLOYMENT CREDIT
Special tax credit has been available for companies in Indian reservations since 2006.

CDC
Companies are encouraged to make gifts or long-term loans to community development corporations (CDCs) in exchange for receiving tax credits. CDCs may serve local areas, often with a high percentage of low-income residents. They may be involved in real estate (affordable housing, for example), education (early years and lifelong), and economic development.

Tax credits continued

7 NEW MARKET CREDIT
Credits are offered for equity investments made in a community development entity.

8 REFORESTATION CREDIT
Aimed at the timber trade, companies receive credit for projects that sponsor reforestation.

9 ALCOHOL FUELS CREDIT
Companies producing or selling alcohol fuels or mixtures such as gasohol or ethanol receive credits.

10 RESEARCH AND DEVELOPMENT CREDIT
This is aimed at encouraging more companies to raise investment on research and experimental activities.

1

REHABILITATION CREDIT
This credit is aimed at encouraging companies to rehabilitate
certified historic buildings.

2

RETIREMENT PLAN START-UP CREDIT
Small employers (with fewer than 100 employees) who set up
retirement plans are now entitled to a tax credit.

3

EMPLOYER-PROVIDED CHILD CARE CREDIT
Small and mid-sized companies are eligible for a tax credit of
25 percent of the qualified child care expenses they provide.

Tax deductions

The best way of lowering your taxable income is to make a list of every legitimate deductible business expense.

GENERAL RULES
There are certain threshold issues to note before filing to make any business deductions.

1 KEEP RECORDS
An IRS agent will want to see thorough records of any expenses to prove that the list of deductions you have made is correct. Records of related information such as income, gains, losses, and costs should also be readily available. Record should be kept for at least four years.

2 PROVIDE RECEIPTS
You will have to provide receipts to prove that the expense ha in fact been paid for. A receipt can include a credit card charge slip or canceled check.

MONITOR EXPENSES

Always check that the expenditure you are claiming is reasonable for your line of business, frequent, ongoing, and a commonly accepted part of your business. Examples include:

- holidays
- gifts and cards to clients
- installation of a business telephone line
- business meals and entertainment

A more comprehensive list of expenses deemed appropriate by the IRS appears on pp. 224–225.

Tax deductions continued

Two categories cause the greatest concern for companies:

1 BUSINESS VS. PERSONAL TRAVEL

What happens when you travel to a destination for business and combine it with personal leisure? Basically, if you travel to a destination and engage in both personal and business activities, you are allowed to deduct your traveling expenses to and from the destination only if the principal reason for the trip is business. If you are principally on vacation, and add in one or two business meetings, that is not a legitimate business travel expense, and cannot be deducted.

MEALS AND ENTERTAINMENT EXPENSES
There are two rules of thumb in the view of the IRS:

■ Is the occasion directly related? Does the meeting take place in a clear business setting? Are you promoting your business during the meal? Are you hoping to derive some income or business benefit as a result of the meal? If you meet in a location like a cocktail lounge, sporting club where other attendees are not present for business purposes, then you cannot claim expenses.

■ Is there a direct association? Is the entertainment associated with the business meeting? For instance, if a meal immediately precedes or follows a key business meeting, the facts surrounding the meeting will be considered and may be approved.

Tax deductions continued

COMMON DEDUCTIBLE EXPENSES

- advertising

- bad debts from sales or services

- bank fees on business accounts

- car and truck expenses

- cost of goods sold

- depreciation

- employee benefits

- gifts to customers and suppliers

- insurance (casualty and liability)

- interest

- legal and professional services

- meals and entertainment

- office expenses

- pension and profit-sharing plans

- rent or lease expense

- repairs and maintenance

- services performed by independent contractors

- supplies and materials (not included in cost of goods sold)

- travel expenses

- utilities

- wages of employees

Tax deductions continued

NONDEDUCTIBLE EXPENSES

The following won't be typically allowed a business expense deduction:

- bar or professional examination fees

- capital expenditures (not fully deductible in the year placed in service, but yearly deductions are allowed to recover the cost of the item over a specified time period)

- charitable contributions or gifts (unless you are operating as a sole proprietor)

- clothing, unless it's specific for the business

- commuting expenses

- estate tax

- federal income tax

- fines and penalties incurred for violations of law such as traffic tickets.

- gift tax; inheritance tax

gifts to employees or business contacts that are valued at more than $25

inheritance tax

job-hunting expenses (for a new trade or business)

life insurance premiums, if the business, or the business owner, is a direct or indirect beneficiary

lobbying expenses

personal, living, or family expenses

political contributions, including tickets to political dinners

tax penalty payments

transfer taxes on business property

Tax during periods of loss

NET OPERATING LOSS

WHAT IS IT?
Net operating loss (NOL) occurs when your business loss exceeds your total income for the year, a scenario that faces many small business owners in the first few years of operation.

For tax purposes, this loss can be used to offset income and reduce taxes in another year. This is an exception to the general income tax rule that stipulates that taxable income is determined on the basis of your current year's events.

This general rule applies principally to sole proprietorships (for other structures, see pp. 192–203).

CARRYBACK/CARRYFORWARD

1 CARRYFORWARD
In the case of a start-up that obviously hasn't paid tax in the past, the S tax code does allow companies to use the present loss and carry it forward to the future. When the company is in profit, these losses can be used to offset tax liabilities.

CARRYBACK

In the case of a company that has been operating for some years and incurs sudden losses, it can use the current loss to offset tax paid in the past, literally carrying them back. The company has to start off carrying the loss to the earliest carryback year although the maximum number of years allowed is two.

LES FOR REPORTING ON NOL FOR NONPROPRIETORSHIPS

PARTNERSHIP

A partnership may not carry the loss backward or forward to other years as a net operating loss but the partners' shares of the loss may result in net operating loss carrybacks or carryovers on their individual tax returns.

C CORPORATION

For these entities suffering net operating loss, there are no tax benefits to the shareholders. The loss can only be used by the corporation itself, for instance by offsetting against the income of its subsidiaries. If a corporation anticipates net operating losses, it can elect to change to S corporation status and pass the losses on to the shareholders (see pp. 194–197).

Key terms

CAPITAL GAINS TAX: tax payable when an investment or business asset is sold at a gain. Rates vary between 8 and 20 percent.

CARRYBACK: the process used when a company uses the current loss to offset tax paid in the past.

CARRYFORWARD: the process used when a company uses a present loss and carries it forward to the future to offset tax liabilities.

CORPORATION: an artificially created legal entity, separate from one or more individuals who created it. Most corporations are managed by appointed or elected officers known as representative management.

S CORPORATION: a hybrid form of corporation that is particularly attractive to small private companies because it has some appealing tax benefits enjoyed by partnerships while still providing business owners with the liability protection of a corporation.

LIMITED LIABILITY COMPANY: a hybrid entity that has the legal protections of a corporation and the advantage of being taxed, like a partnership, only once.

LIMITED LIABILITY PARTNERSHIP: a partnership comprised of licensed professionals such as attorneys, accountants, and architects. The partners are liable for their own actions, but not those of the other partners.

NET OPERATING LOSS: describes company losses that exceed a company's total income.

PARTNERSHIP: a business form created when two or more persons get together in a business enterprise for profit.

- General partnership: all partners share in the management of the entity and share in the entity's profits and are also personally liable for its debts.

- Limited partnership: as in a general partnership, the general partners are managers of the enterprise and liable for debts while the limited partners provide capital and get a share in the profits but don't get involved with the management of the company.

SEC: The U.S. Securities and Exchange Commission.

SOLE PROPRIETORSHIP: describes the act of owning a company or business ownership on your own.

TAX CREDITS: these are tax payments taken away from a company's tax bill, applicable only to certain sectors like energy, leisure, and entertainment.

TAX DEDUCTIONS: legitimate deductible business expenses subtracted from a company's income.

KEY TERMS

How are businesses taxed?

1 SOLE PROPRIETORSHIP
WHAT IS IT? You are the sole owner and file annual tax returns on a Schedule C or Schedule C-EZ.
PRO: Faster and less expensive than other types of tax returns.
WATCH OUT: You have unlimited personal liability for anything that goes wrong in your business.

2 PARTNERSHIP
WHAT IS IT? This is created when two or more persons get together i a business enterprise for profit.
PRO: Don't have to pay minimum taxes required of corporations and LLCs
WATCH OUT: Owners are subject to unlimited personal liability for the debts, losses and liabilities of the business.

3 CORPORATION
WHAT IS IT? A corporation (known as C corporation) is considered an artificially created legal entity that exists apart from one or more individuals who created it.
PRO: Shareholders are not legally liable for the corporation's actions.
WATCH OUT: Any profits passed on to shareholders are taxed twice.

S CORPORATIONS

WHAT IS IT? A hybrid form of corporation that is particularly attractive to small private companies.

PRO: It is exempt from corporate tax liability, avoiding the dreaded double taxation. Shareholders are only taxed on their individual tax returns.

WATCH OUT: S corporations can only issue common stock, making it more difficult to raise capital than for a C corporation.

LIMITED LIABILITY COMPANIES

WHAT IS IT? An LLC is a hybrid entity that can be formed as long as the business is not banking, insurance, and certain professional service operations.

PRO: They enjoy pass-through taxation, which allows the income or loss generated by the company to be reflected on owners or shareholders' personal income tax returns.

WATCH OUT: Two people at least are required to form an LLC while one person can form an S corporation. Also, stock of S corporations is freely transferable, while the interest (ownership) of LLCs is not.

Conclusion

Finance is an area in which many managers feel uncomfortable, or even overwhelmed, yet few of a manager's day-to-day decisions do not involve making some manner of financial decision.

Whether you are ordering office supplies or green-lighting the building of a multimillion dollar production facility, many of the concepts you have to understand are essentially the same. This book should have given you the knowledge and confidence to act upon the financial data placed in front of you.

Technology moves on at an ever-increasing speed, and new industries and businesses emerge to take advantage of these change It can be difficult to keep pace. What underpins all business, however, is the importance of knowing what comes in and what goes out of the company in terms of finance and other quantifiable resources. This book has offered an overview of six of the most important areas relating to financ where managers frequently find themselves with something of a knowledge deficit.

ur business has to prepare
ccounts for tax purposes; you have
 be able to read, although not
ecessarily prepare, a balance sheet;
nd you need to understand the
nportance of a budget to the
ccess of any project. Attracting
vestment is crucial for a
usiness's survival and the
ossibilities presented here should
elp you attract the right financing
 the right time. How you "read"
nancial data can aid enormously in
cision making. Finally Chapter 6
s given a basic overview of tax
d taxation.

This book is not intended to replace
the finance professionals in your
organization, but it will enable you
to speak to them effectively, and
hear what they are telling you. As is
the case with many disciplines,
when you understand the key
terminology, you are well on the
way to working effectively with the
concepts. Financial terms are not
difficult, but many do have precise
meanings. A feature of this book
has been the summaries of key
terms at the end of every chapter to
provide a quick, look-up facility
before a meeting or presentation.